SPIROGLYPHICS COLORING BOOK

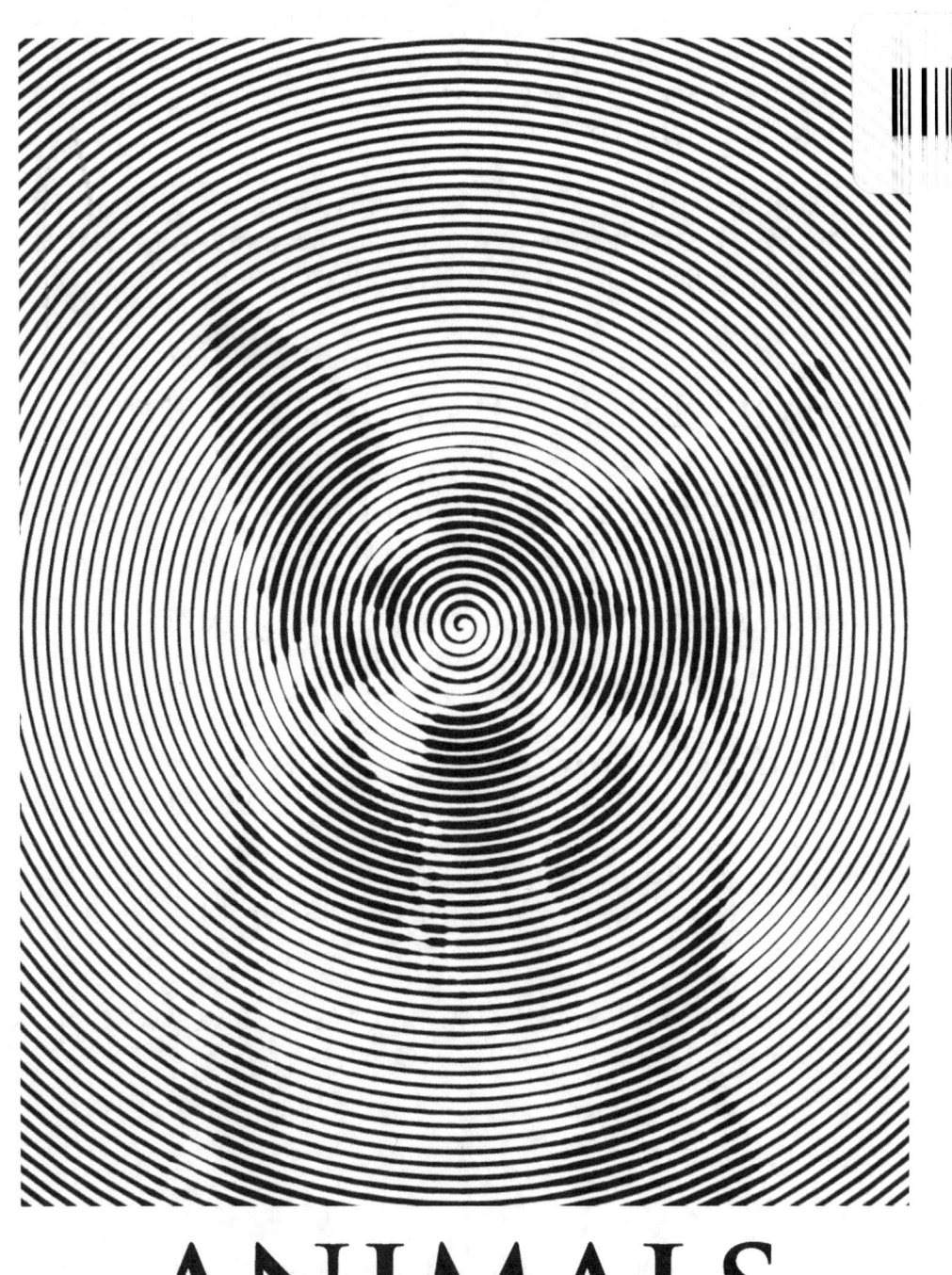

ANIMALS

Bright-Ideas Paper Publishing
Amazon.com/author/bright-ideas
Bright.IdeasPaperPublishing@gmail.com

Enjoy beautiful and relaxing patterns with this easy coloring book from us, Bright-Ideas Paper Publishing

Our coloring book is a wonderful way to show your love of animals while your stress fades away. Each animal features simple patterns which allow you to effortlessly fill pages with any of your favorite colors. We have also included close-up animal portraits and full-body animal designs so you will have plenty of options of what to color next.

You get to color a variety of fun animals designs from this book. You can color each page with realistic colors or let your imagination run wild and use whichever colors you choose!

Why You Will Love this Book?

Relaxing Coloring Pages. Every page you color will pull you into a relaxing world where your responsibilities will seem to fade away…

Beautiful Illustrations. We've included unique images for you to express your creativity and make masterpieces. Which colors will you choose for this book?

Single-sided Pages. Every image is placed on its own backed page to reduce the bleed-through problem found in other coloring books.

Great for All Skill Levels. You can color every page however you want and there is no wrong way to color (even if you are a beginner).

Makes a Wonderful Gift. Know someone who loves to color? Make them smile by getting them a copy too. You could even color together!

NOTE:

Get creative! Don't worry so much about mistakes! We always provide printable copy of each page if you need. Send your requirements to us by email.

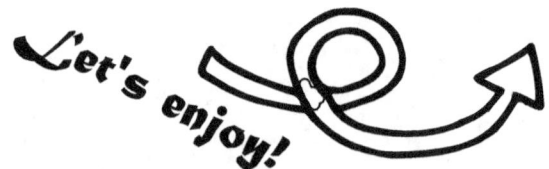

This book belong to

_____

- OTHER BOOKS -

ONE COLOR DOTS LINES SERIES

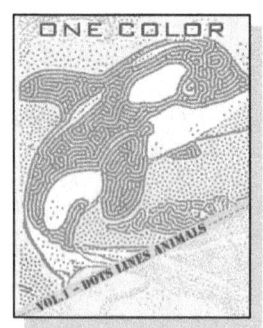 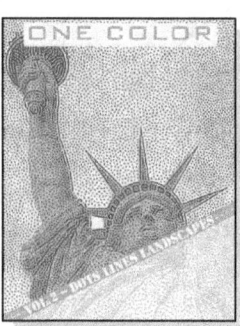 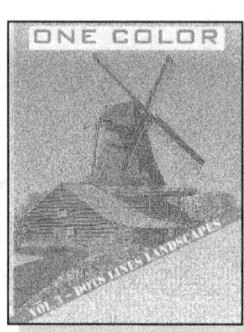 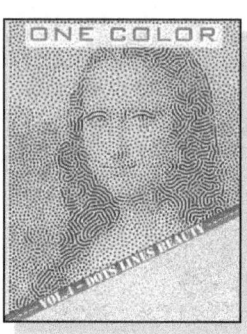 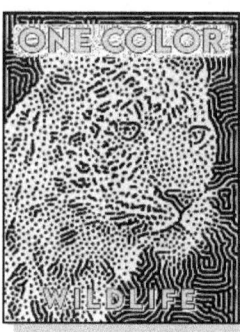

Vol. 1   Vol. 2   Vol. 3   Vol. 4   WILDLIFE

DOTS LINES SPIRAL

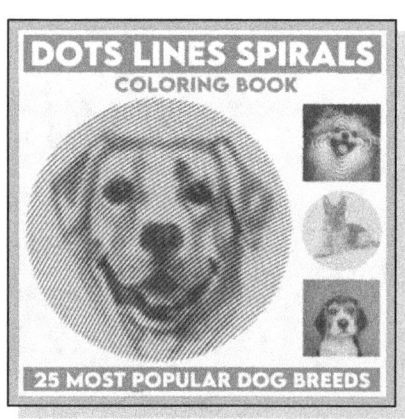 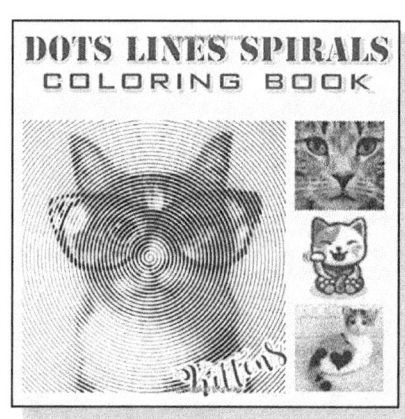 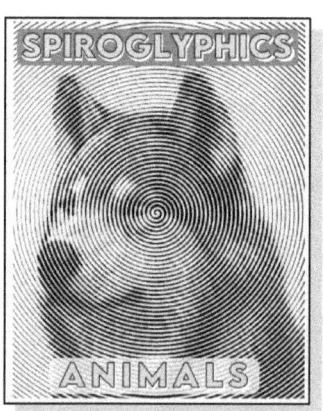

And so on...

Bright-Ideas Paper Publishing
Amazon.com/author/bright-ideas

Coloring test page

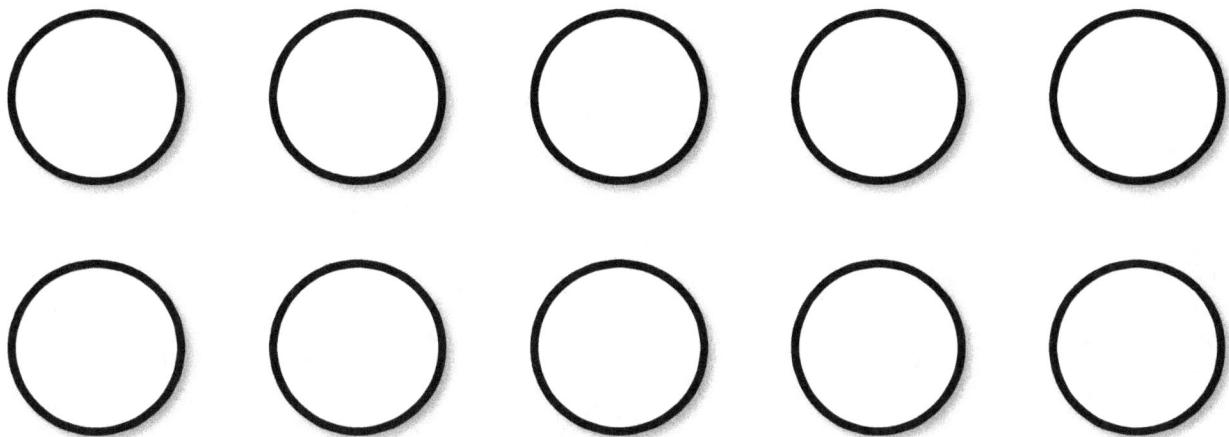

- GUIDE -

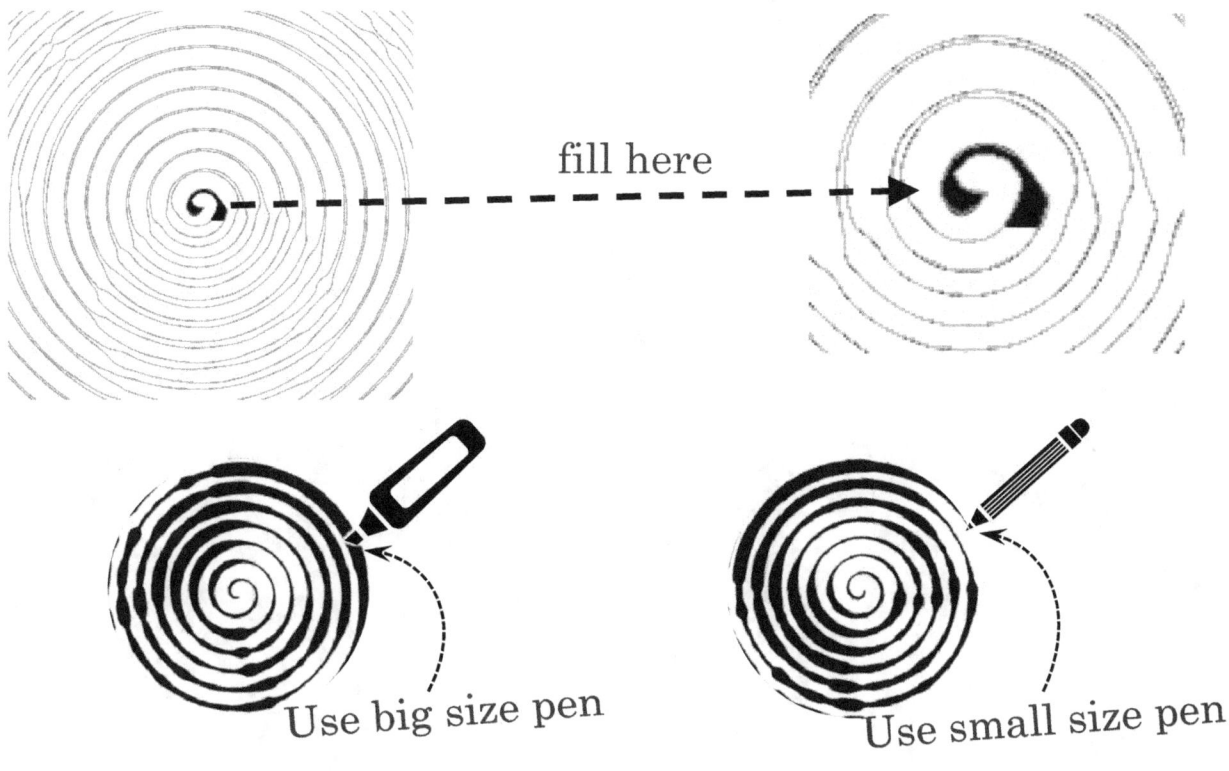

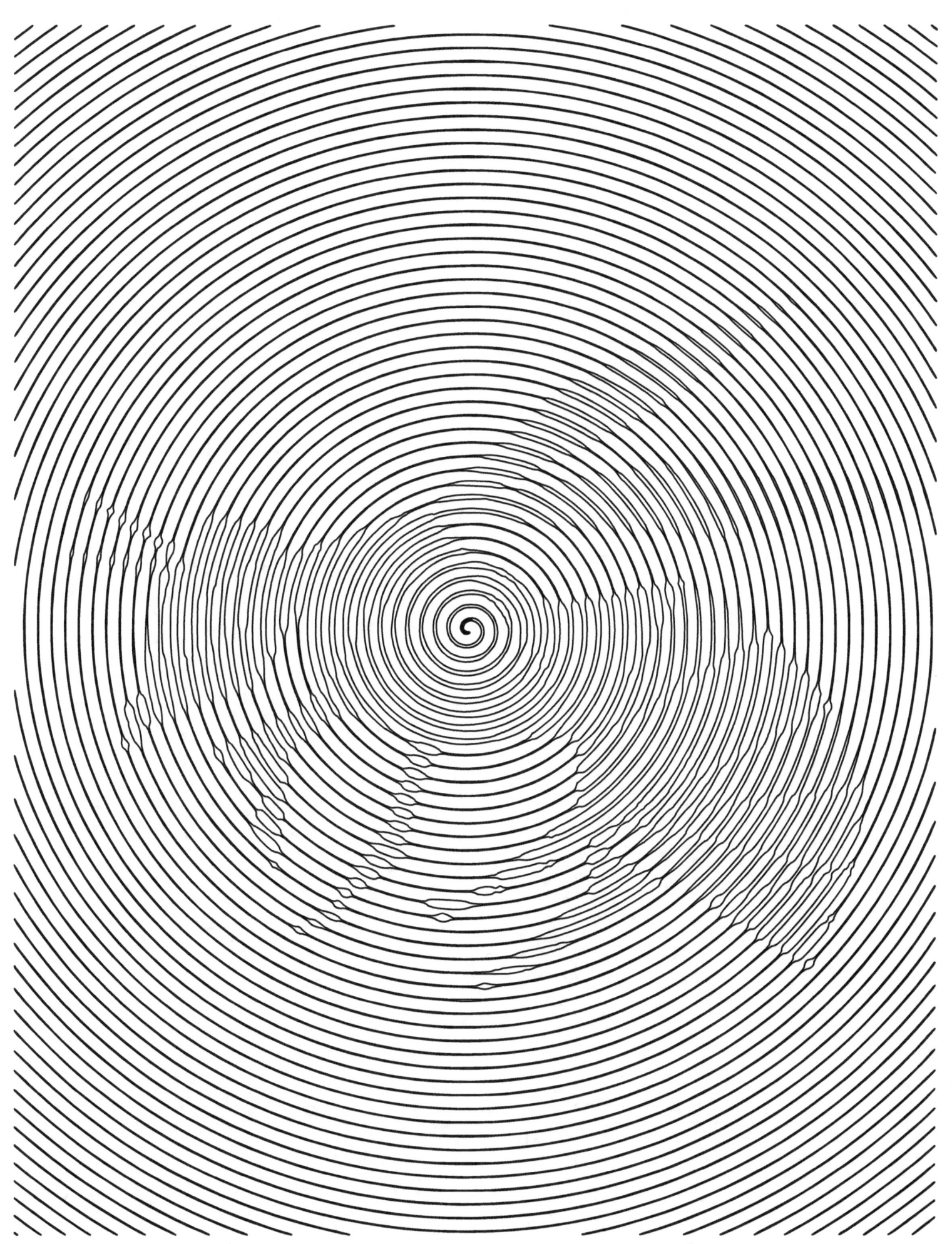

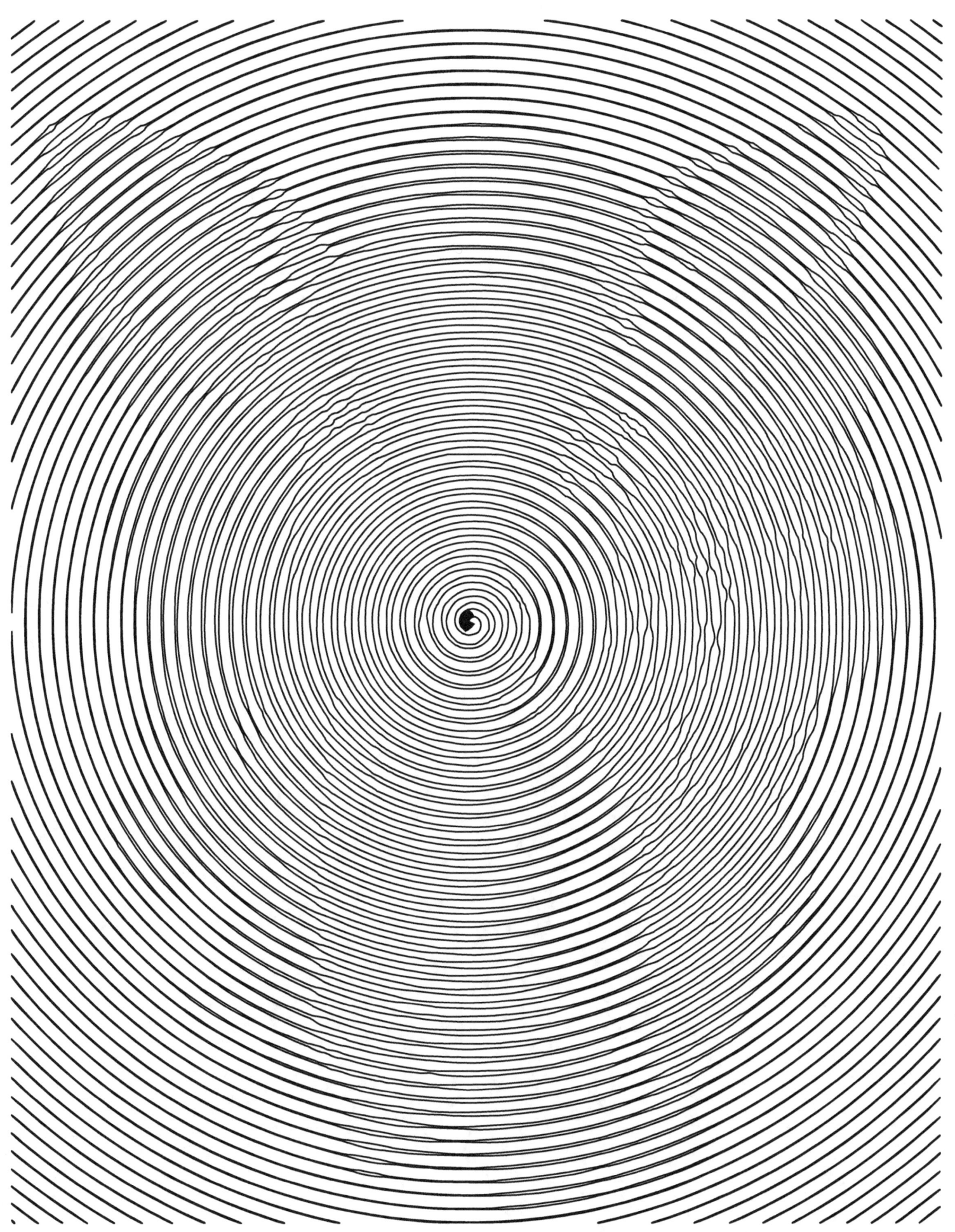

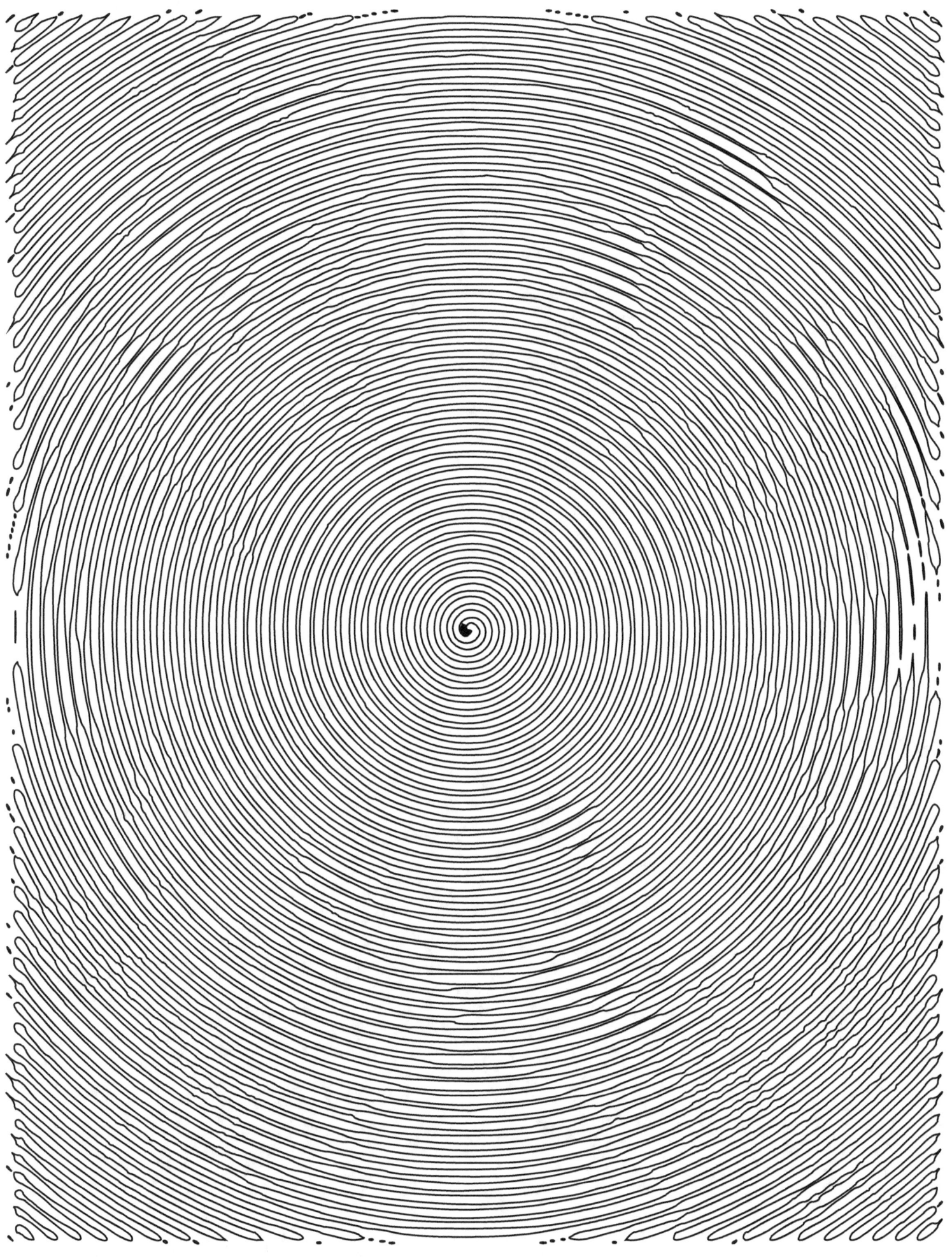

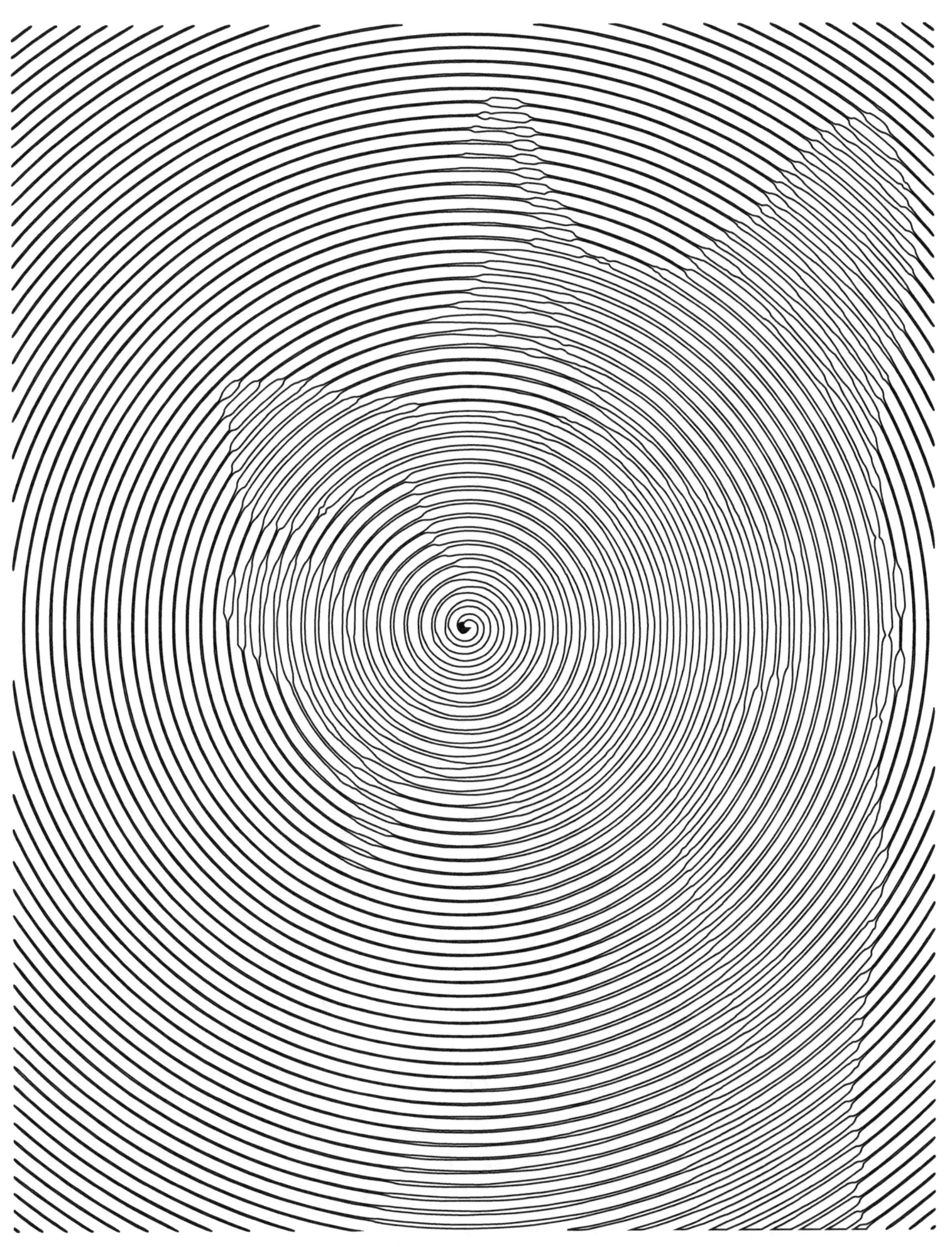

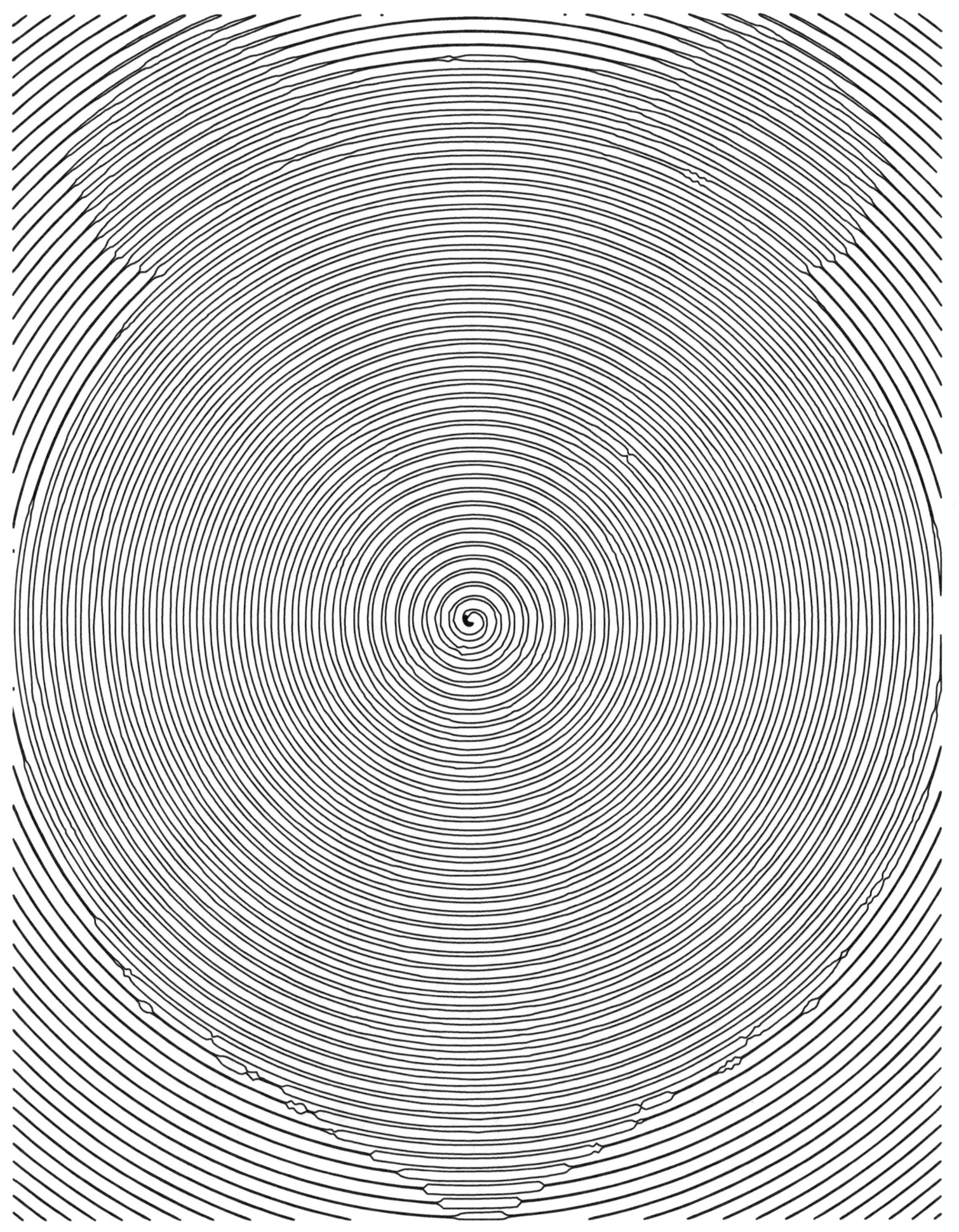

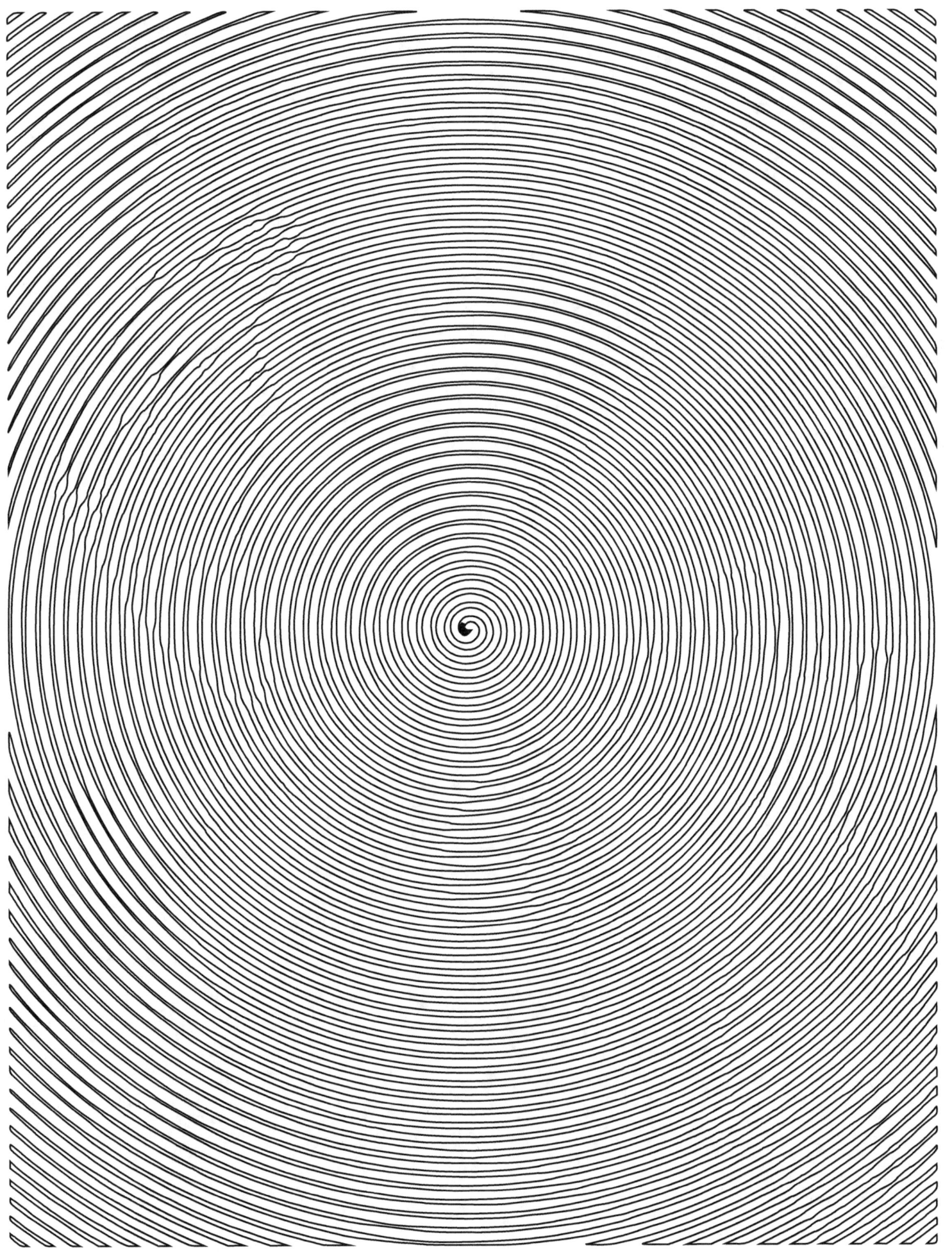

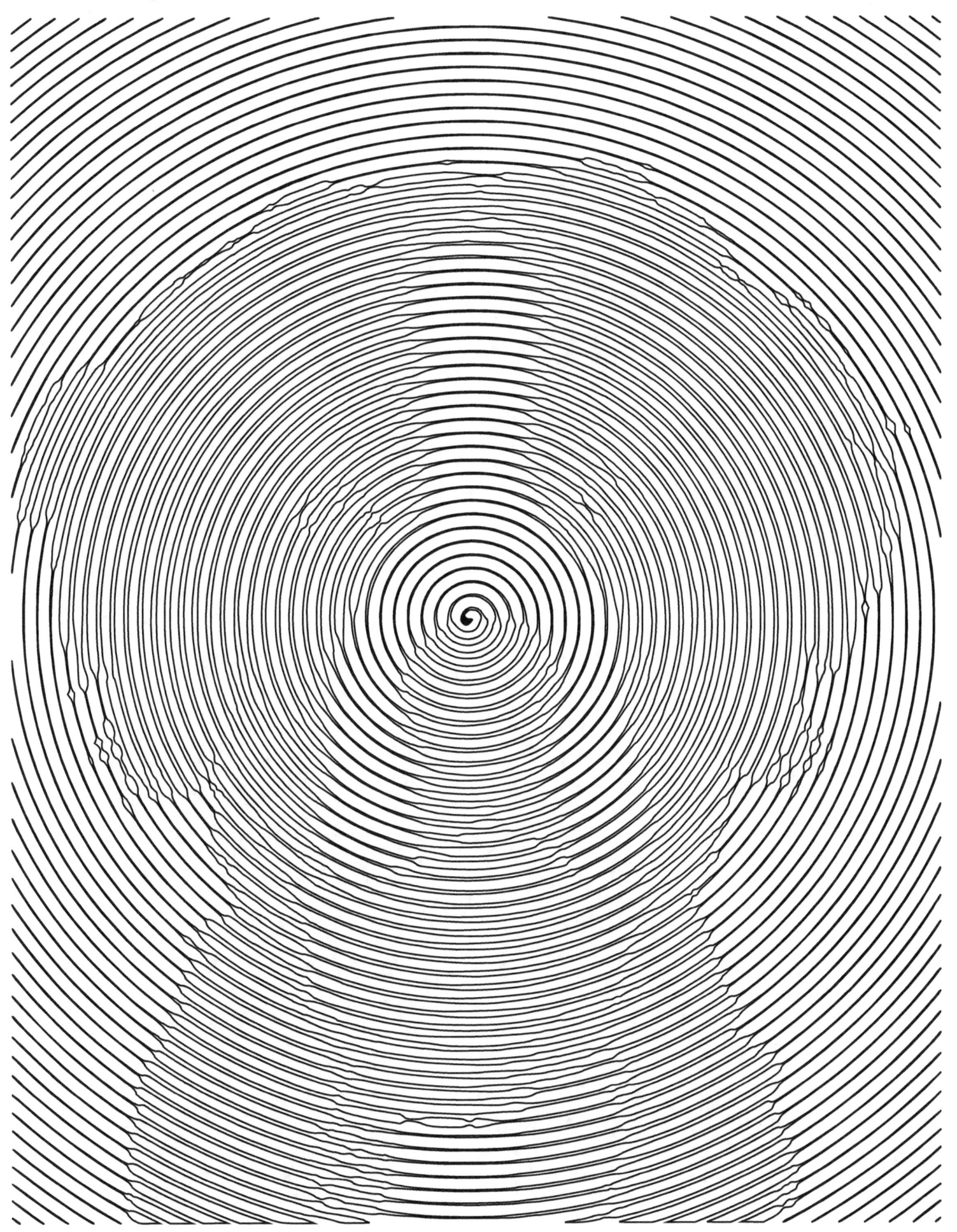

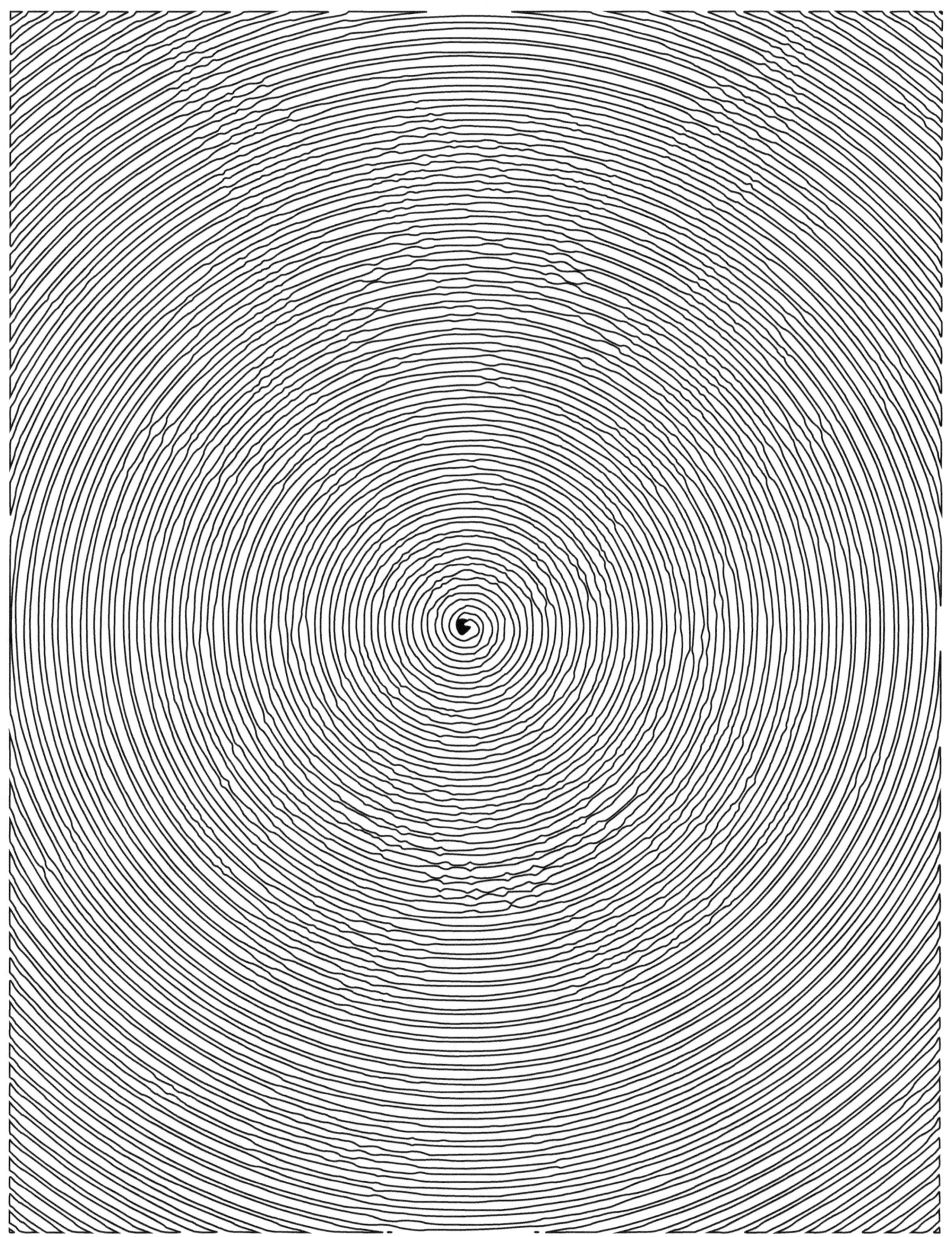

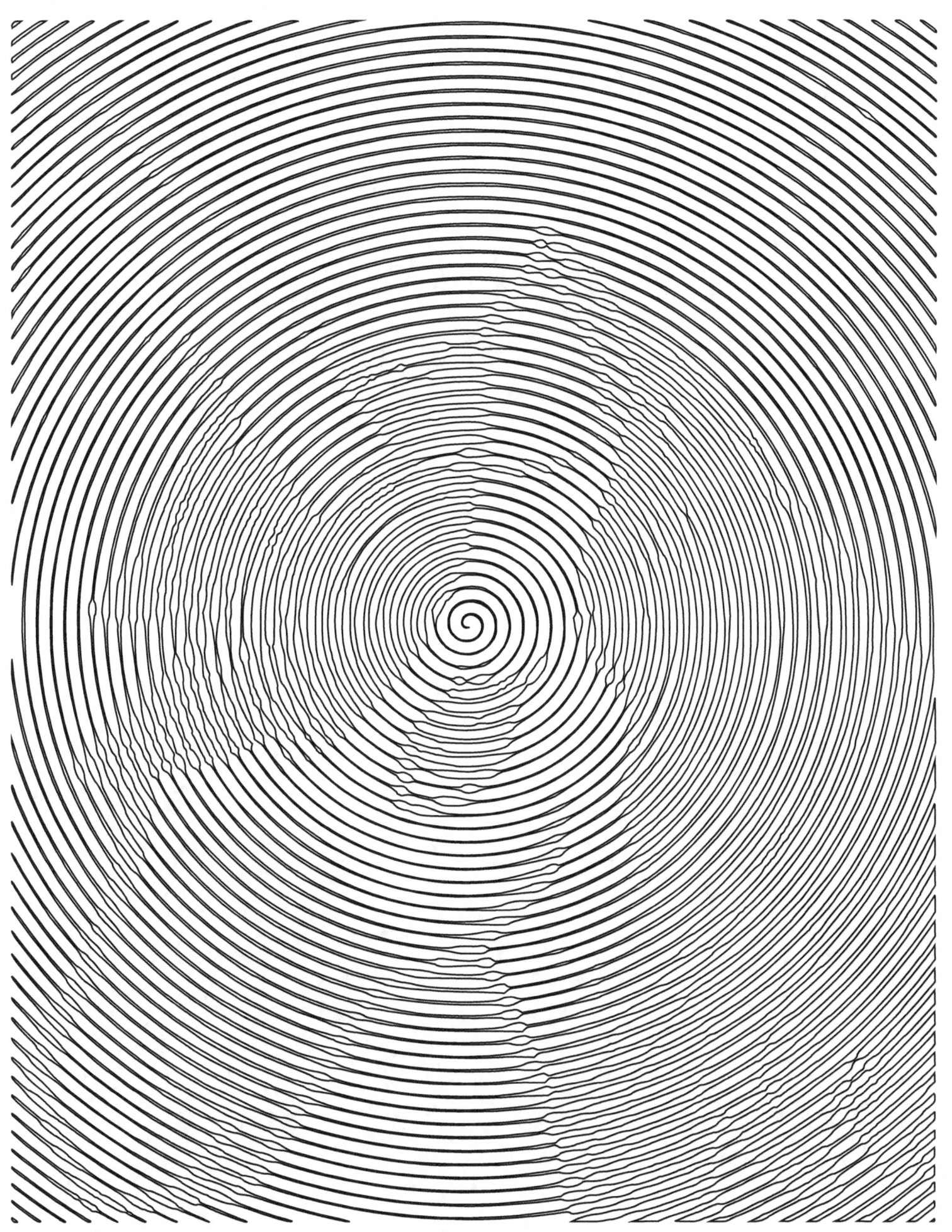

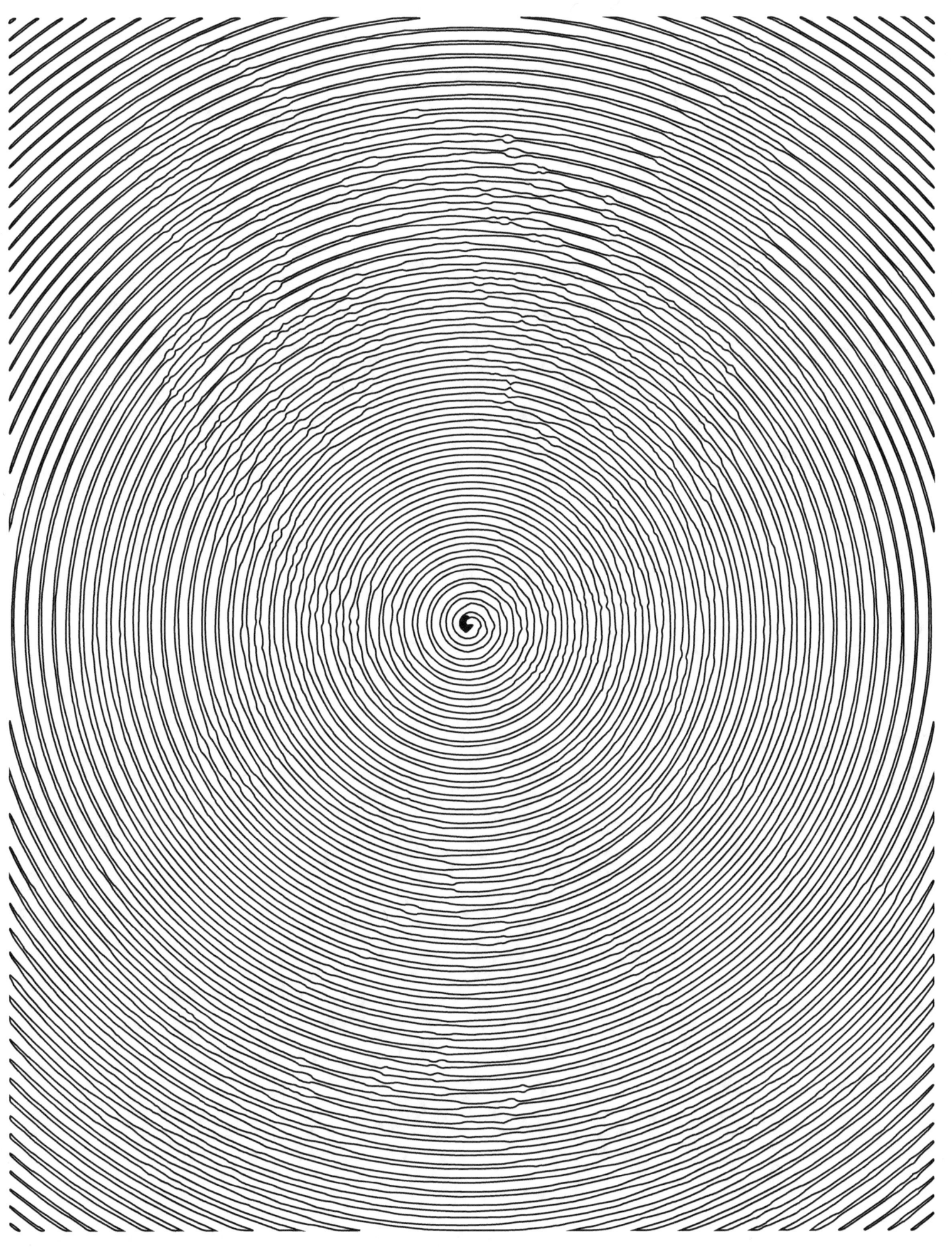

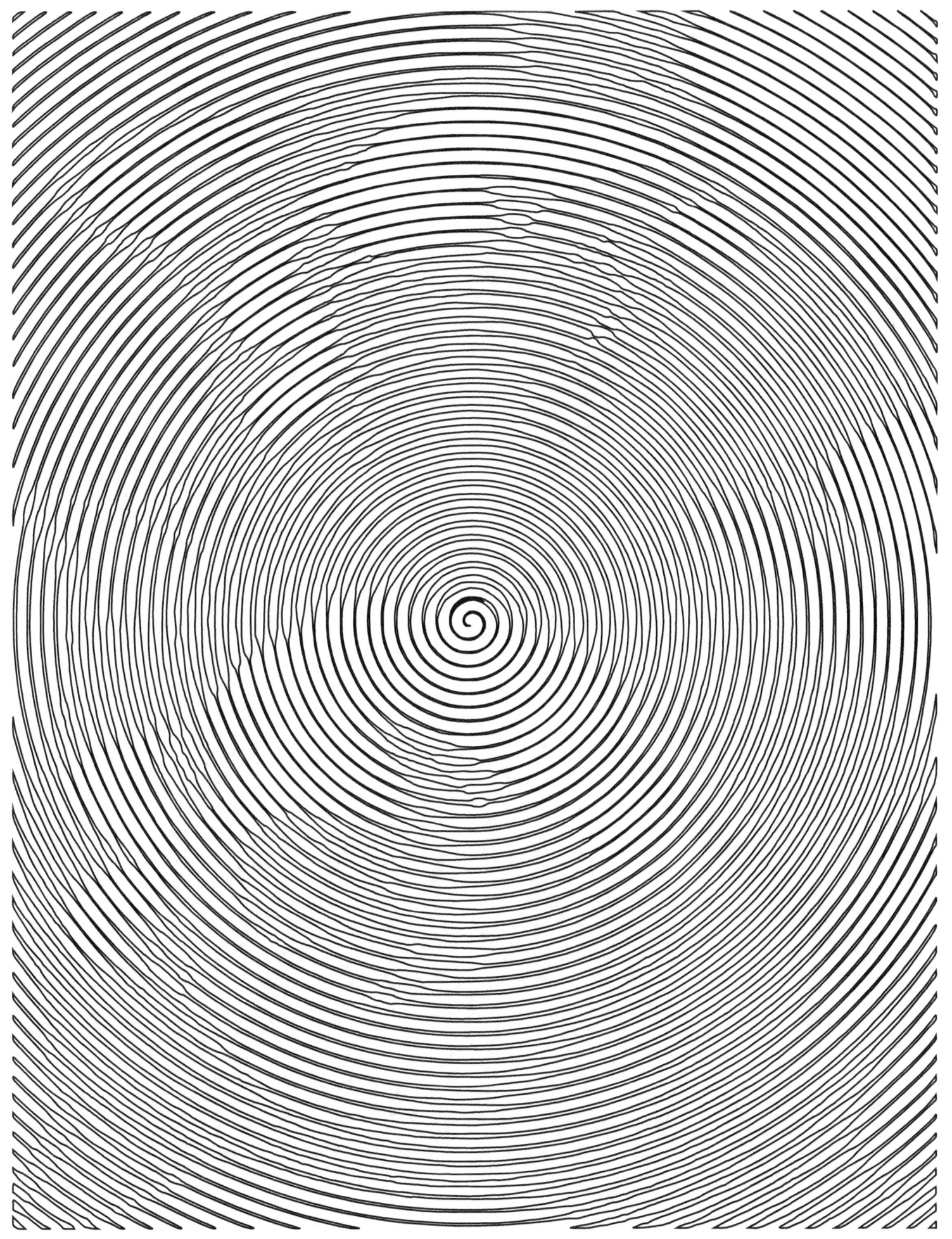

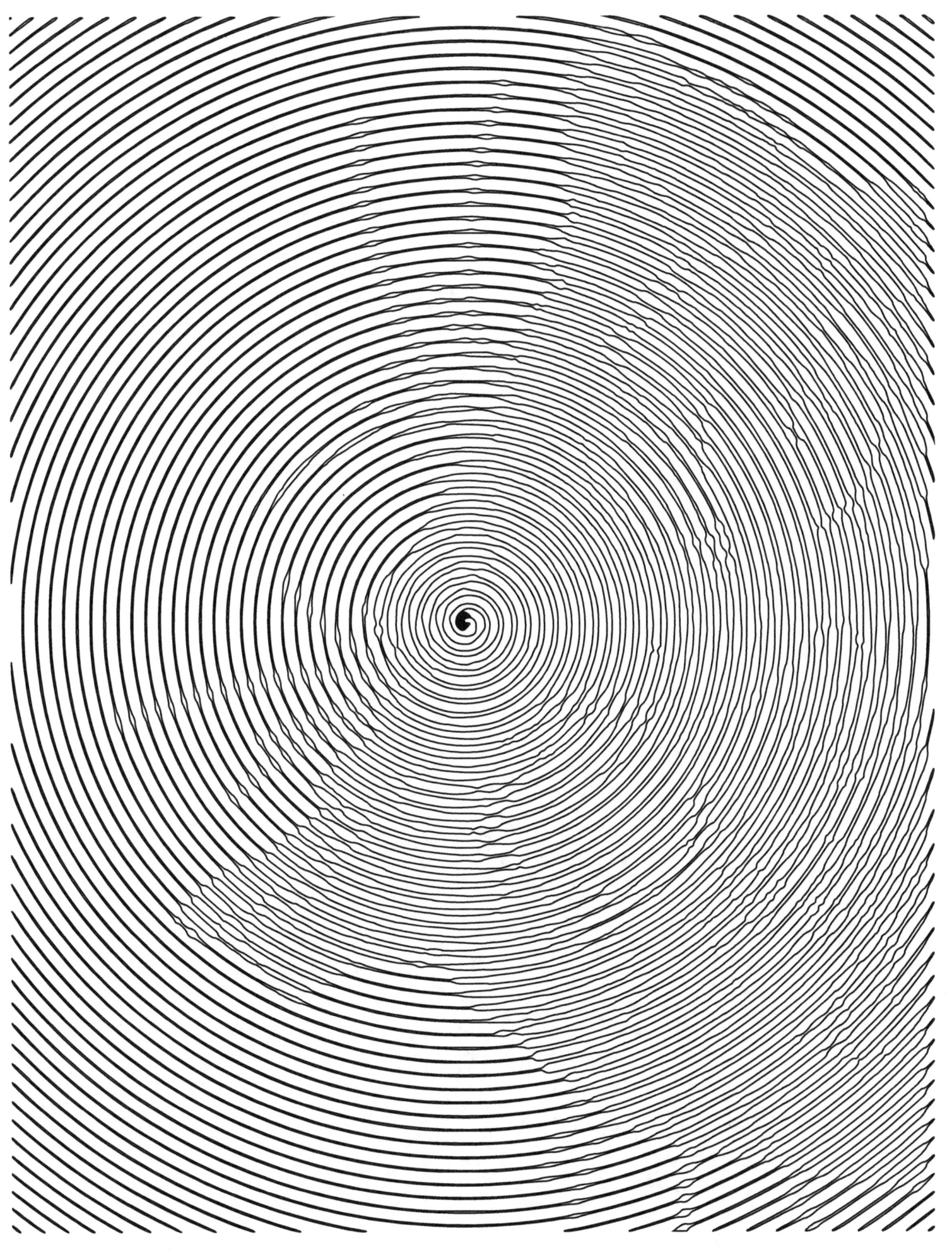

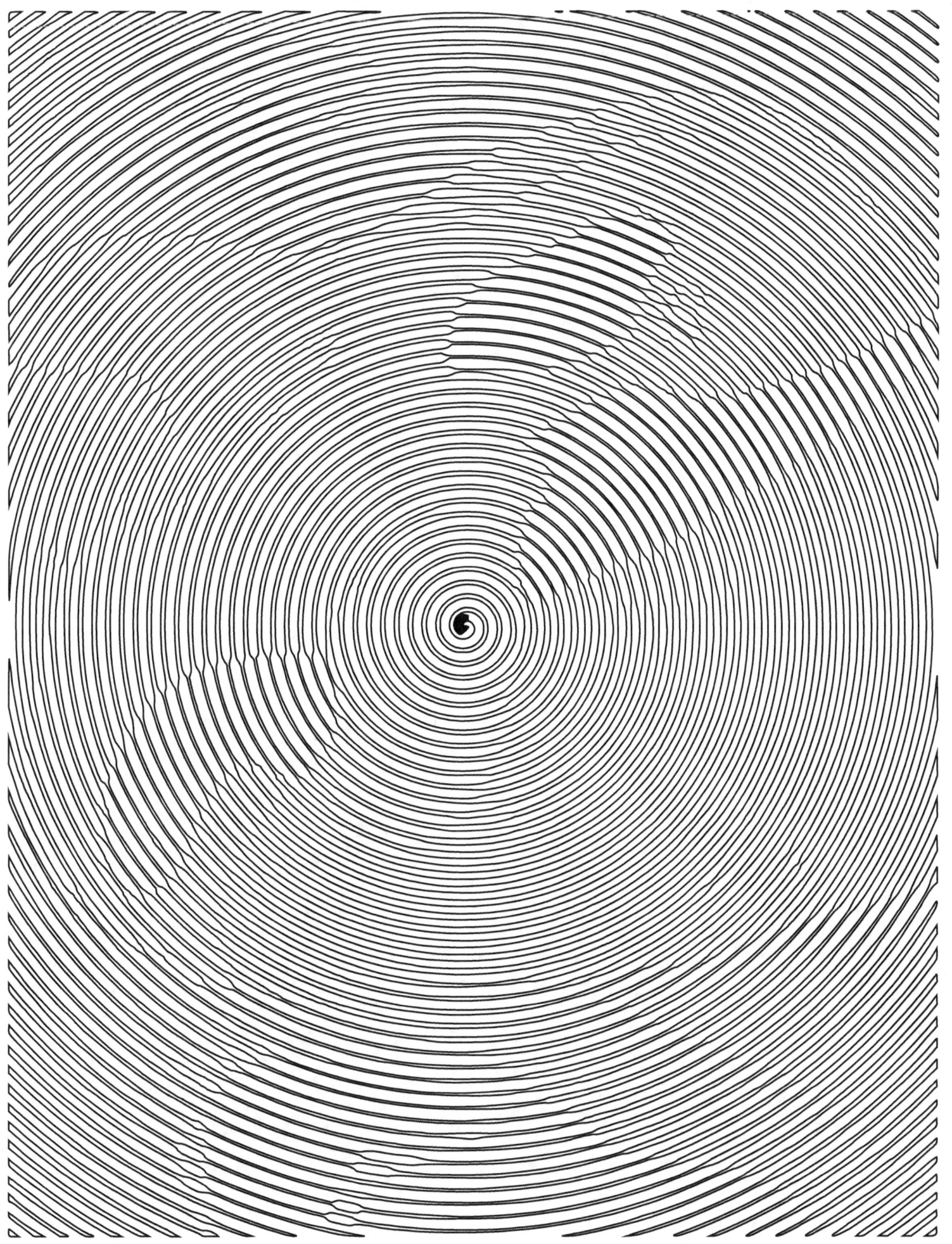

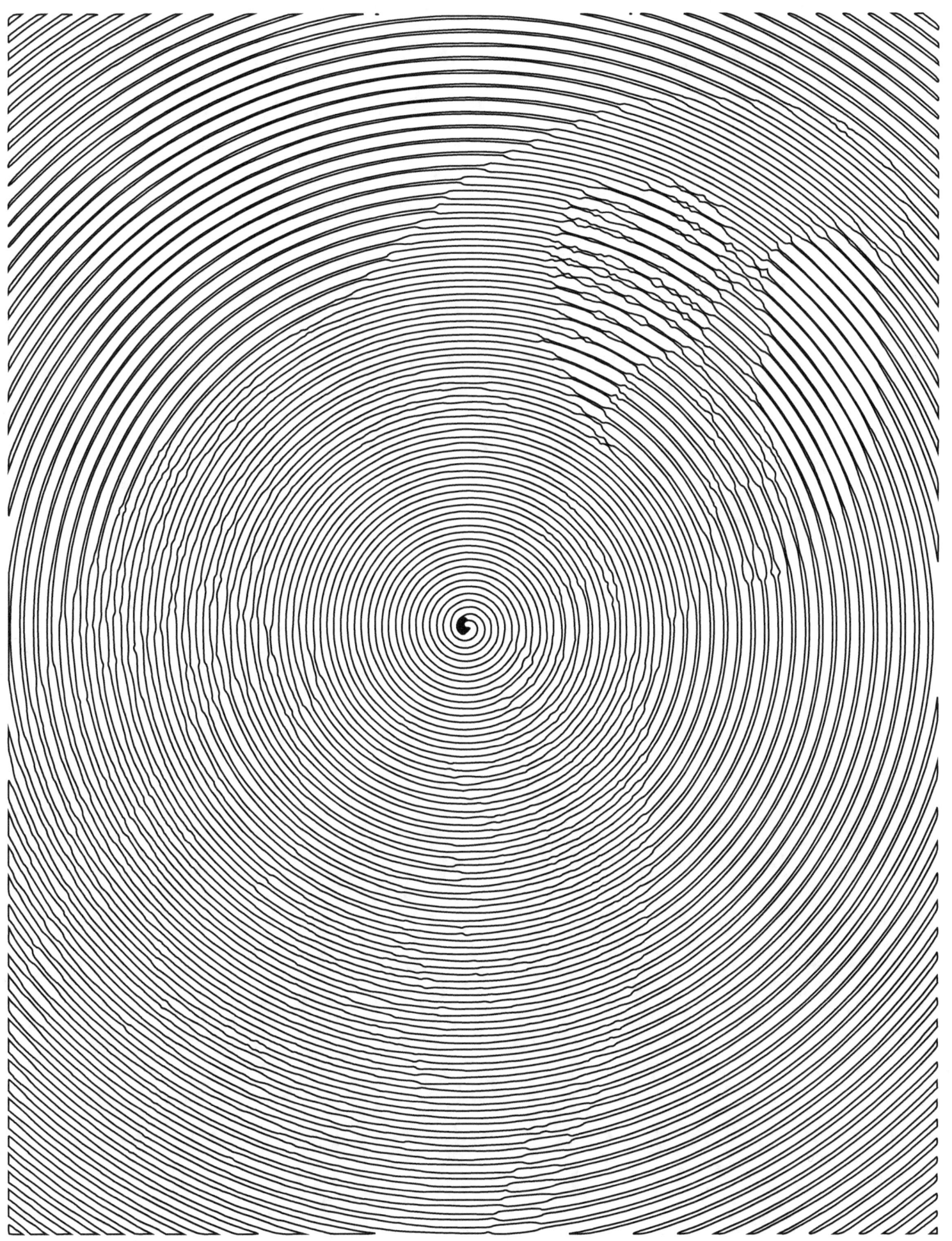

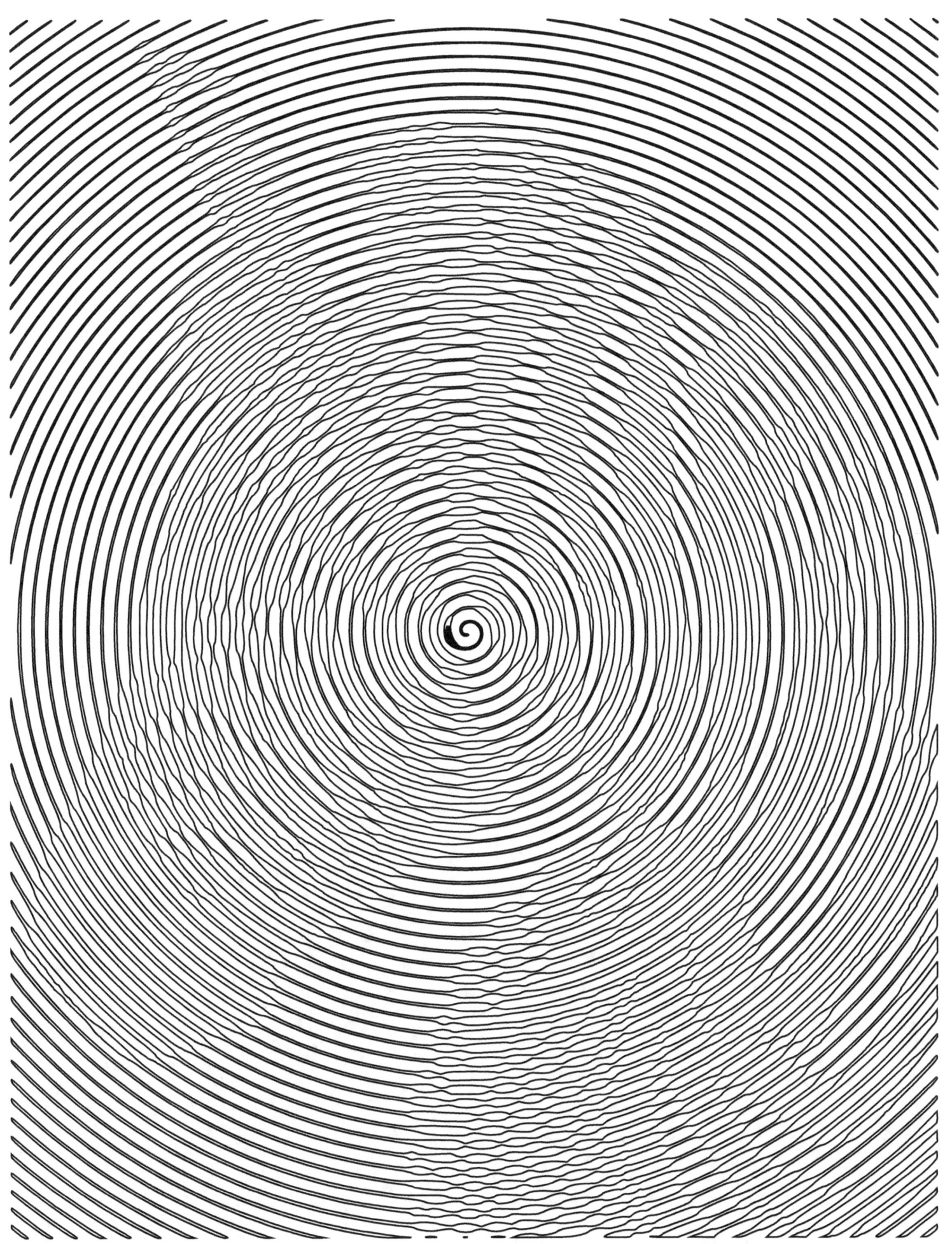

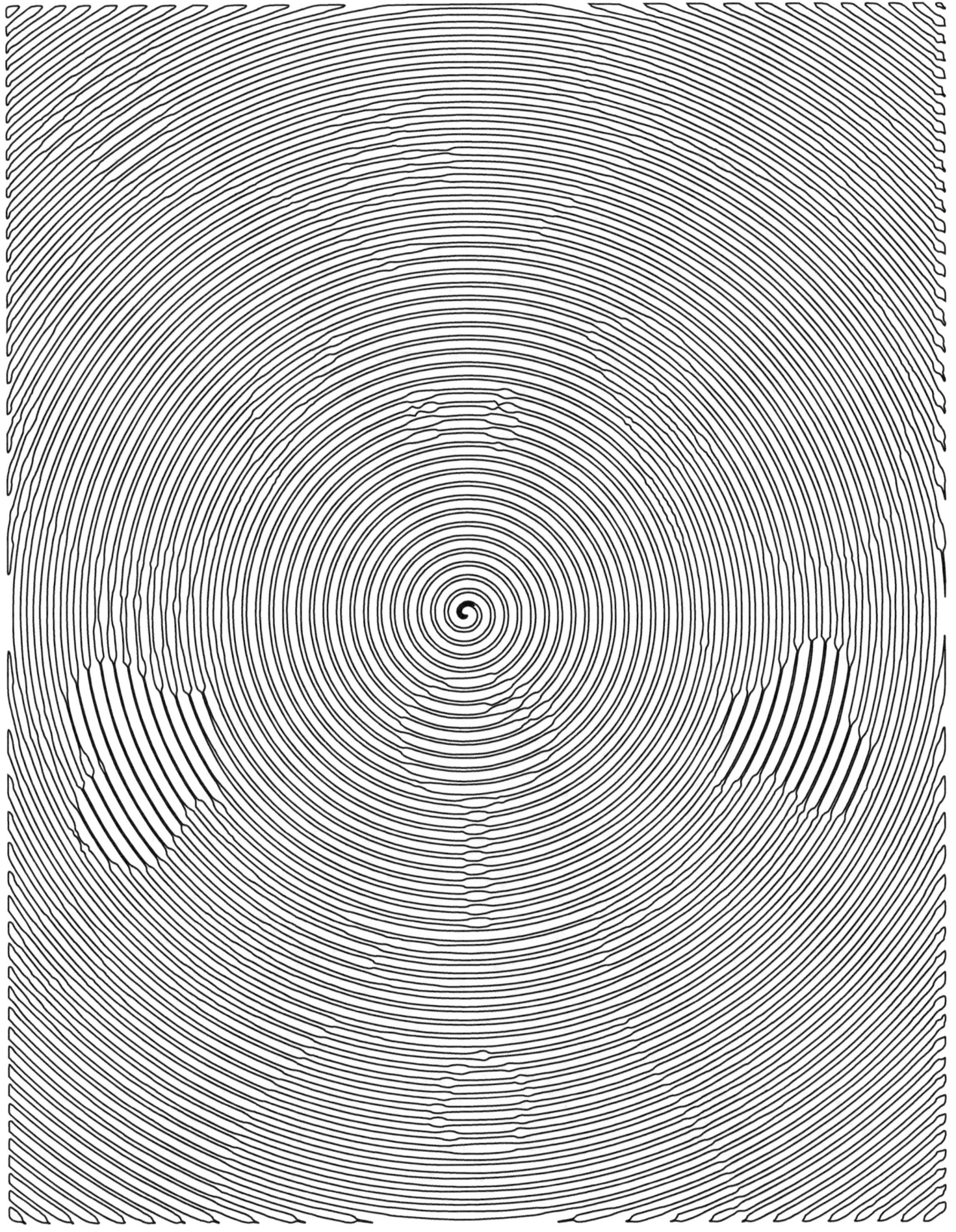

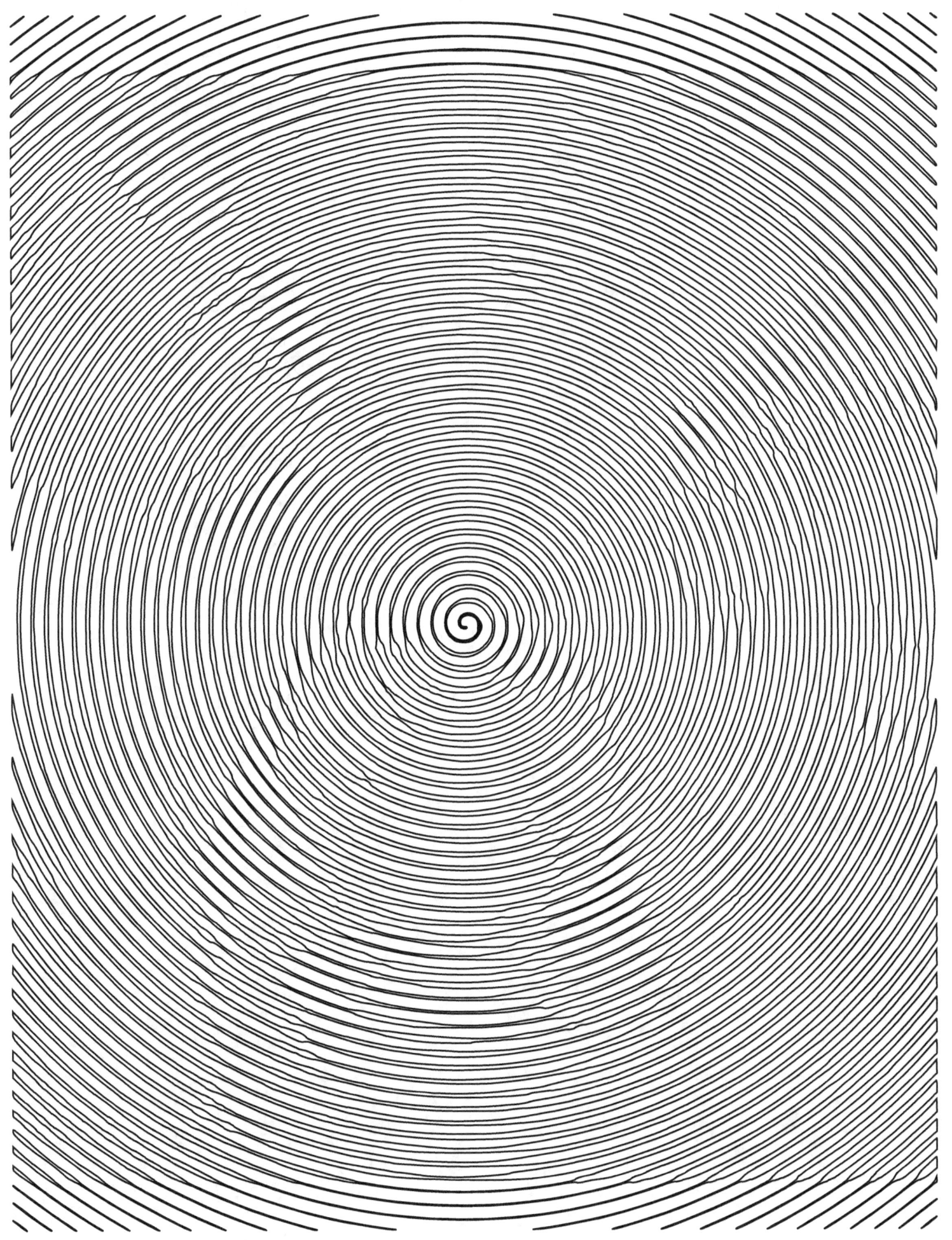

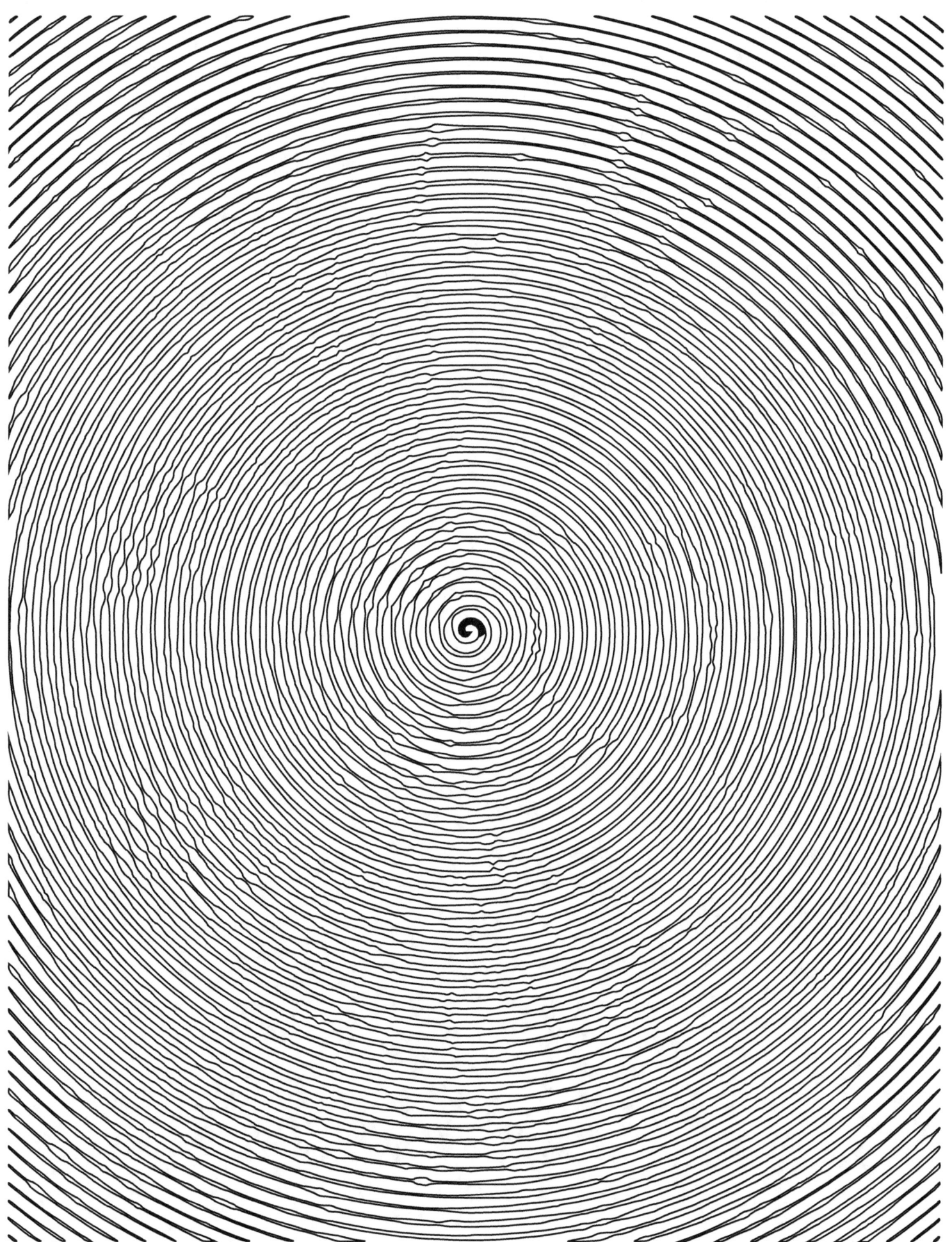

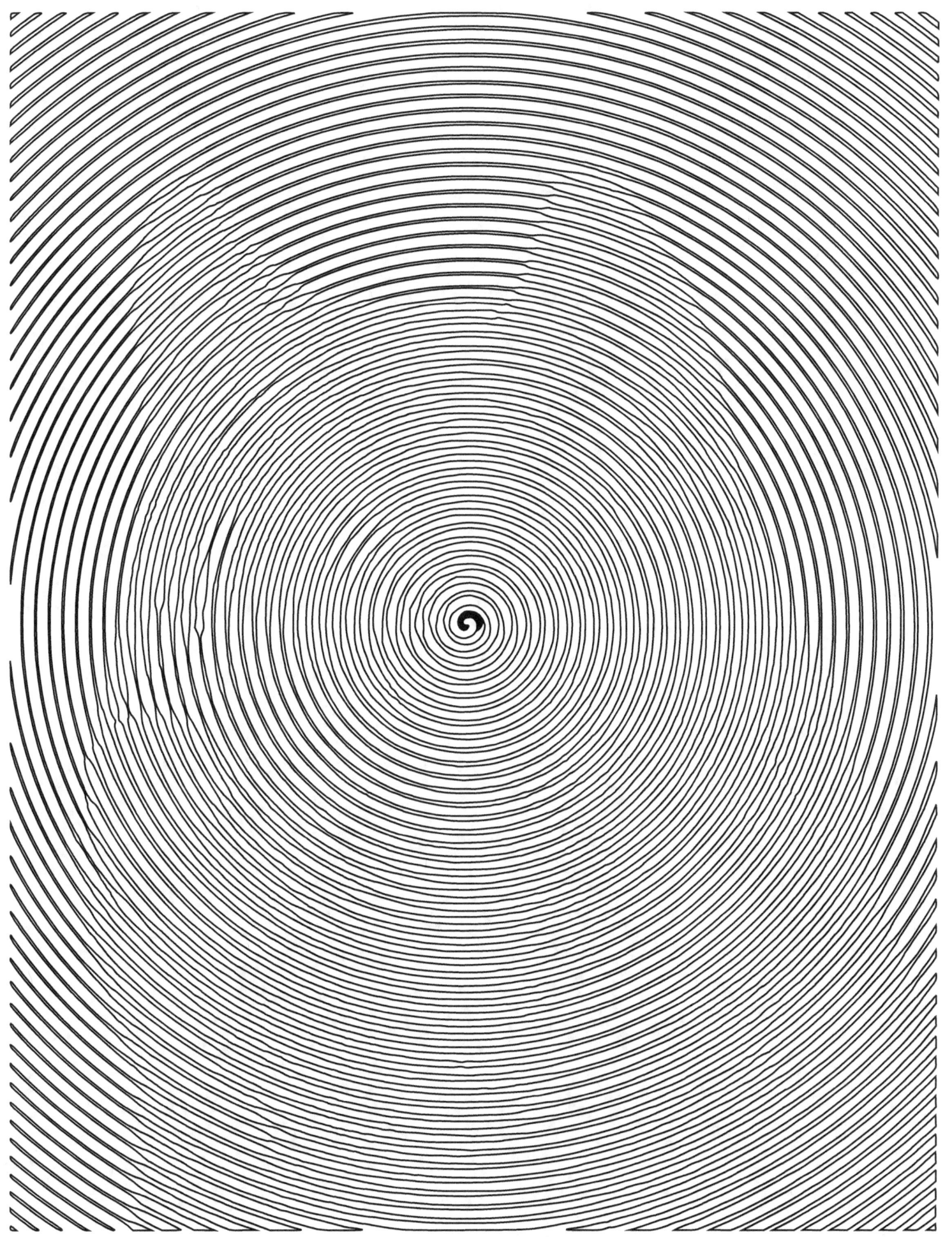

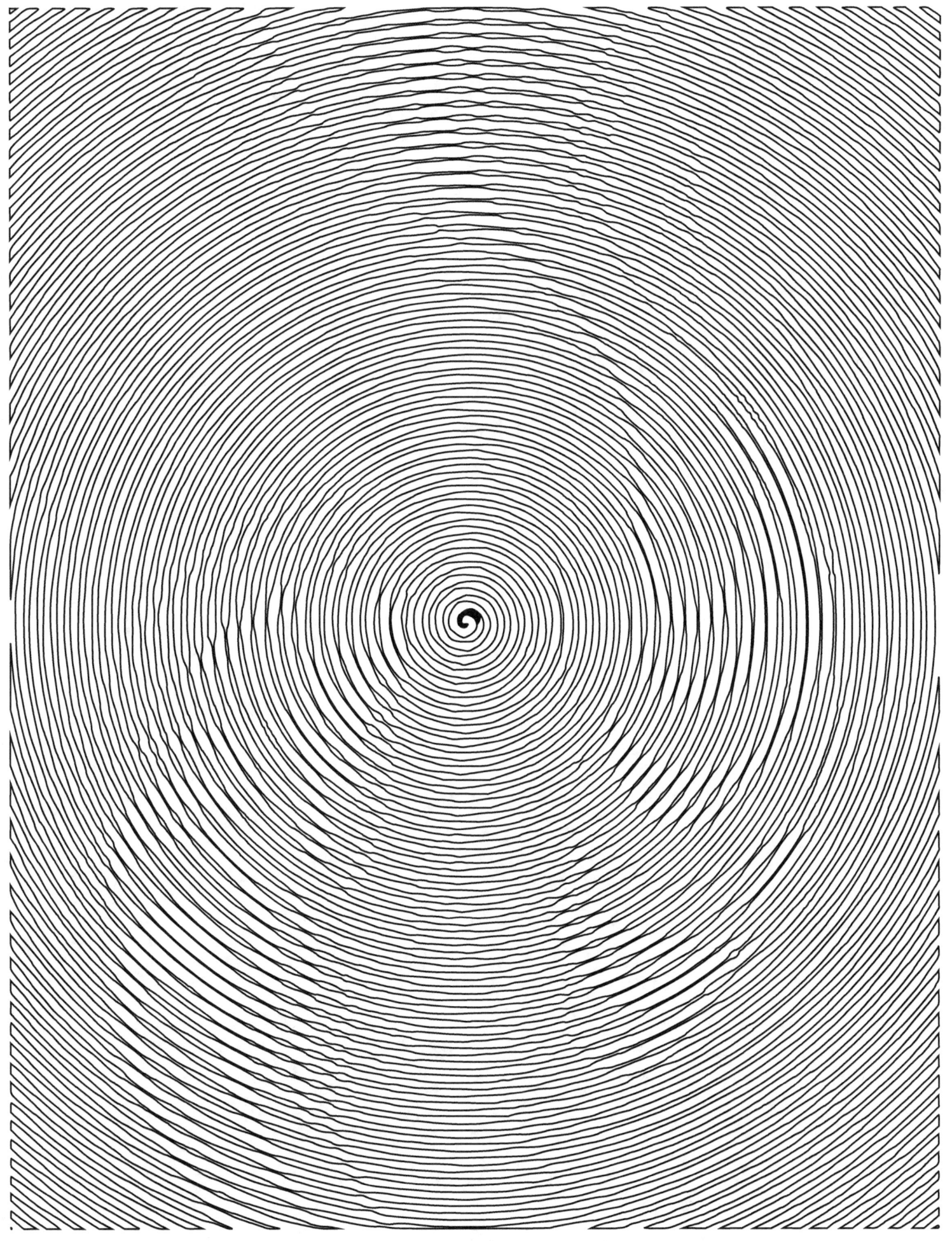

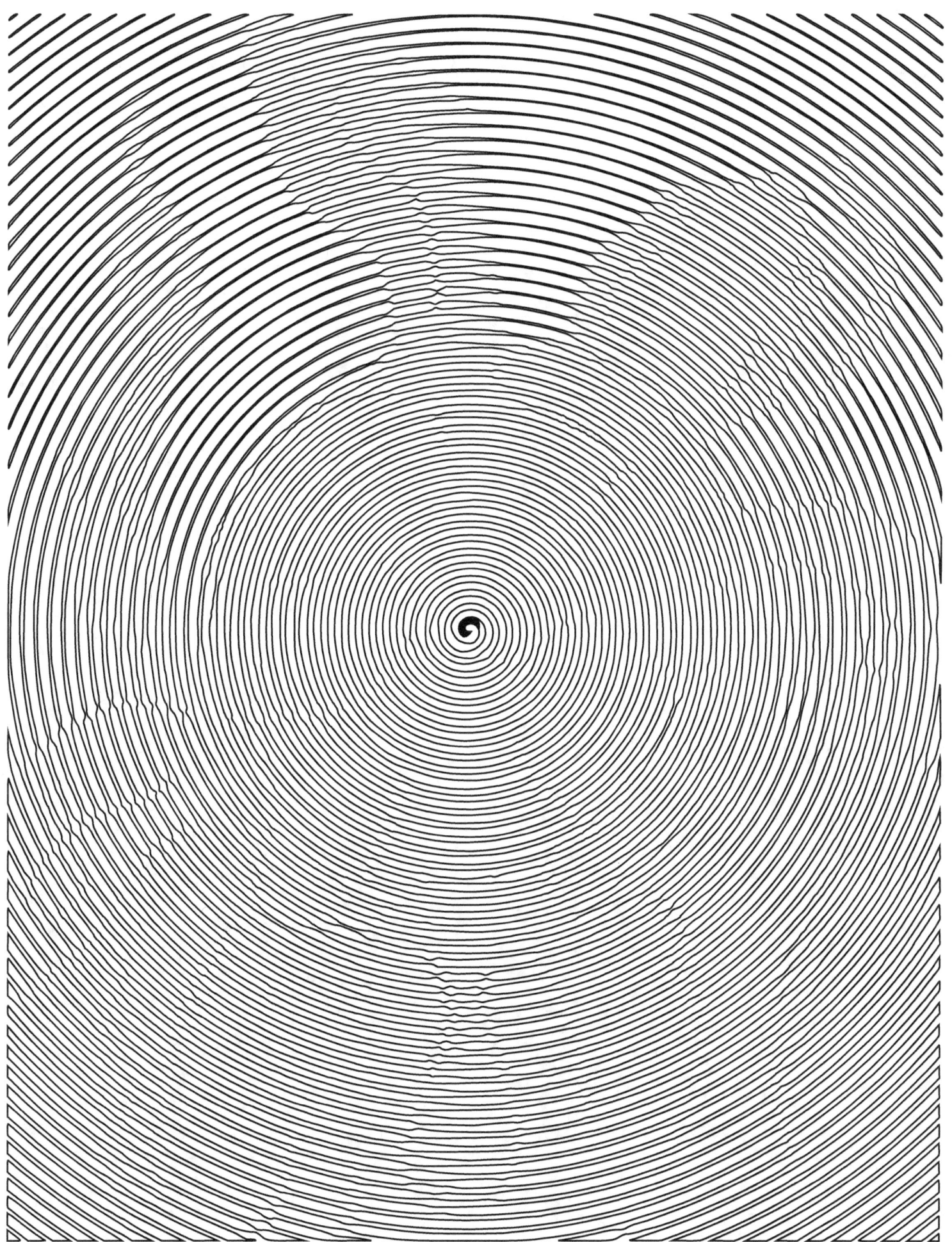

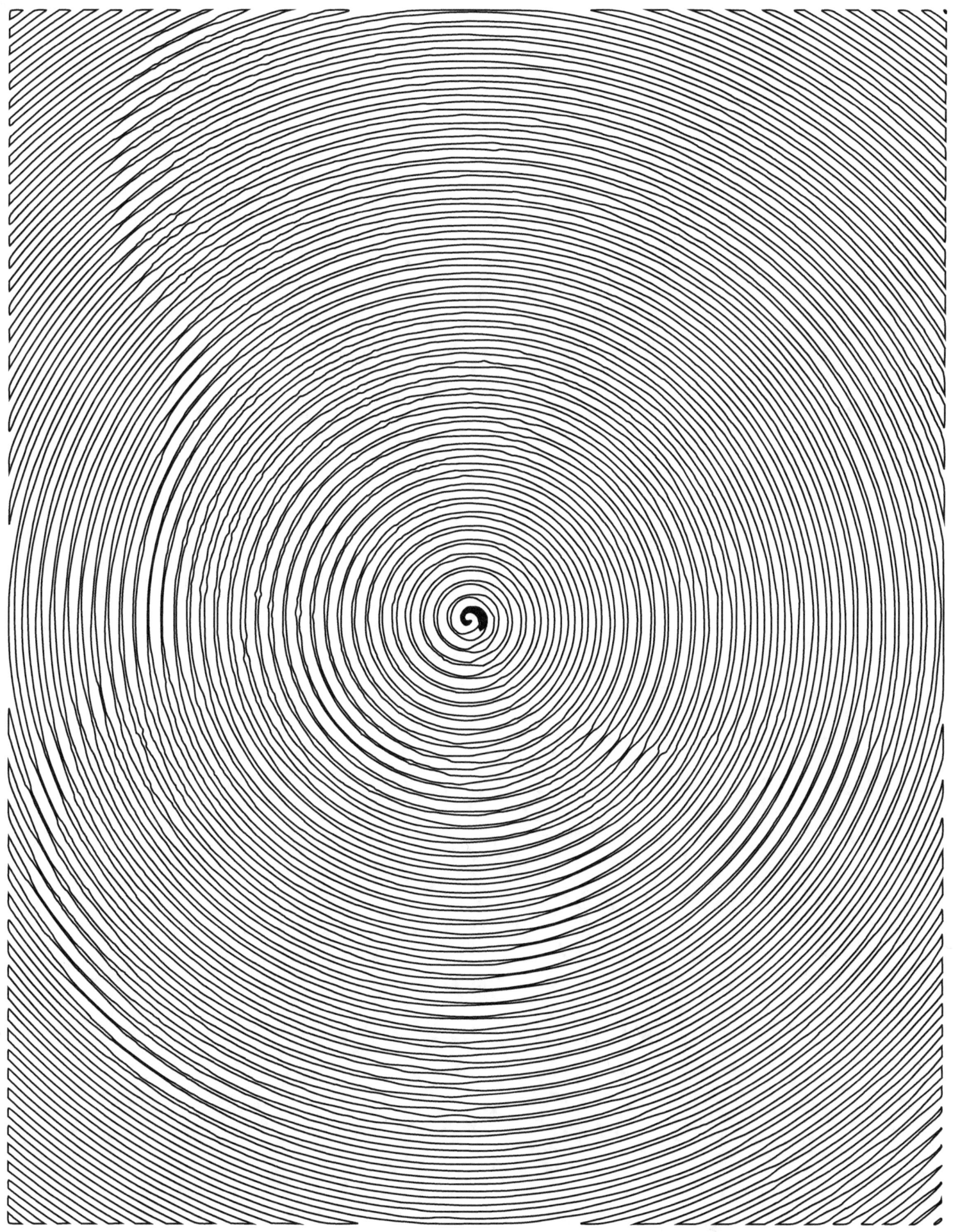

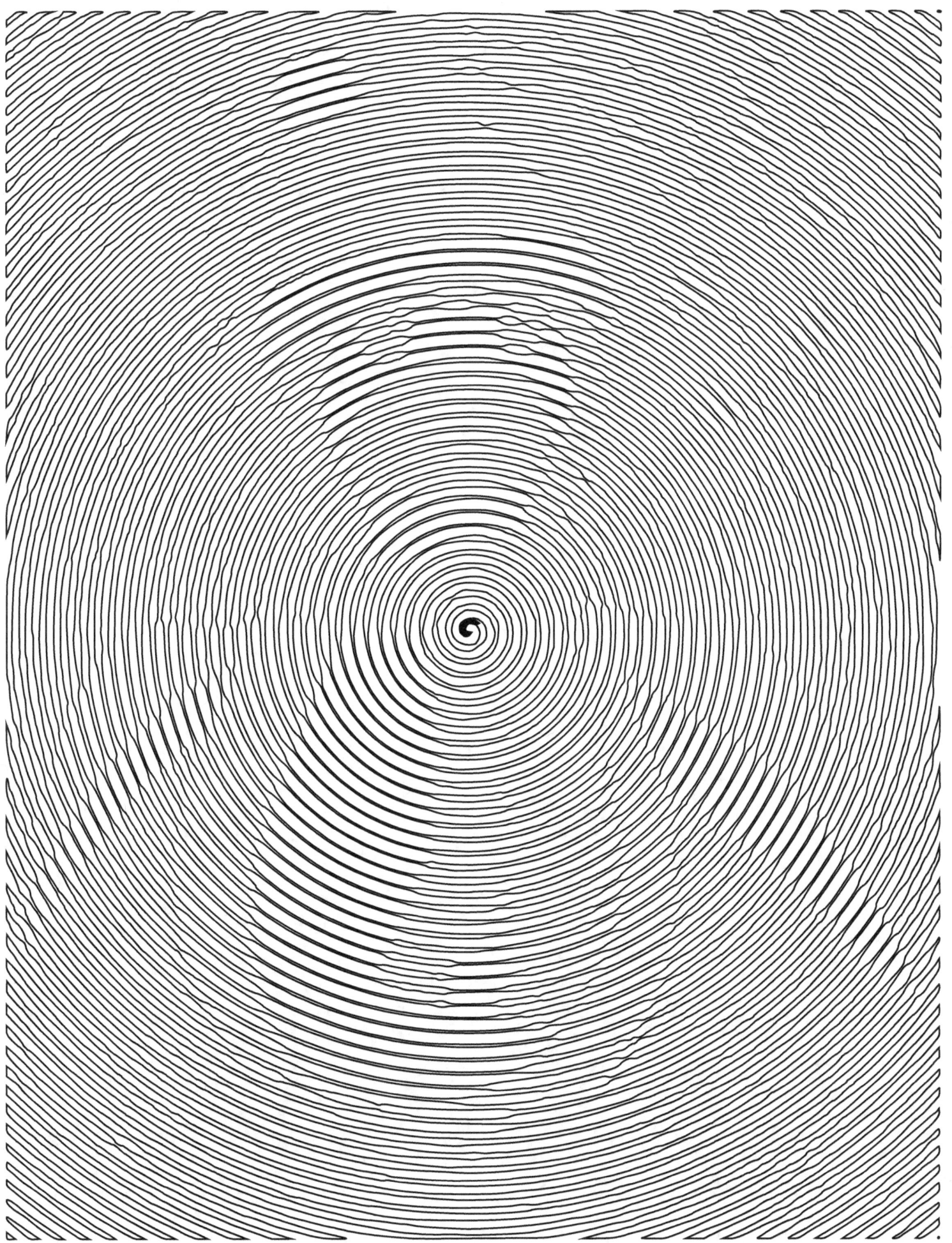

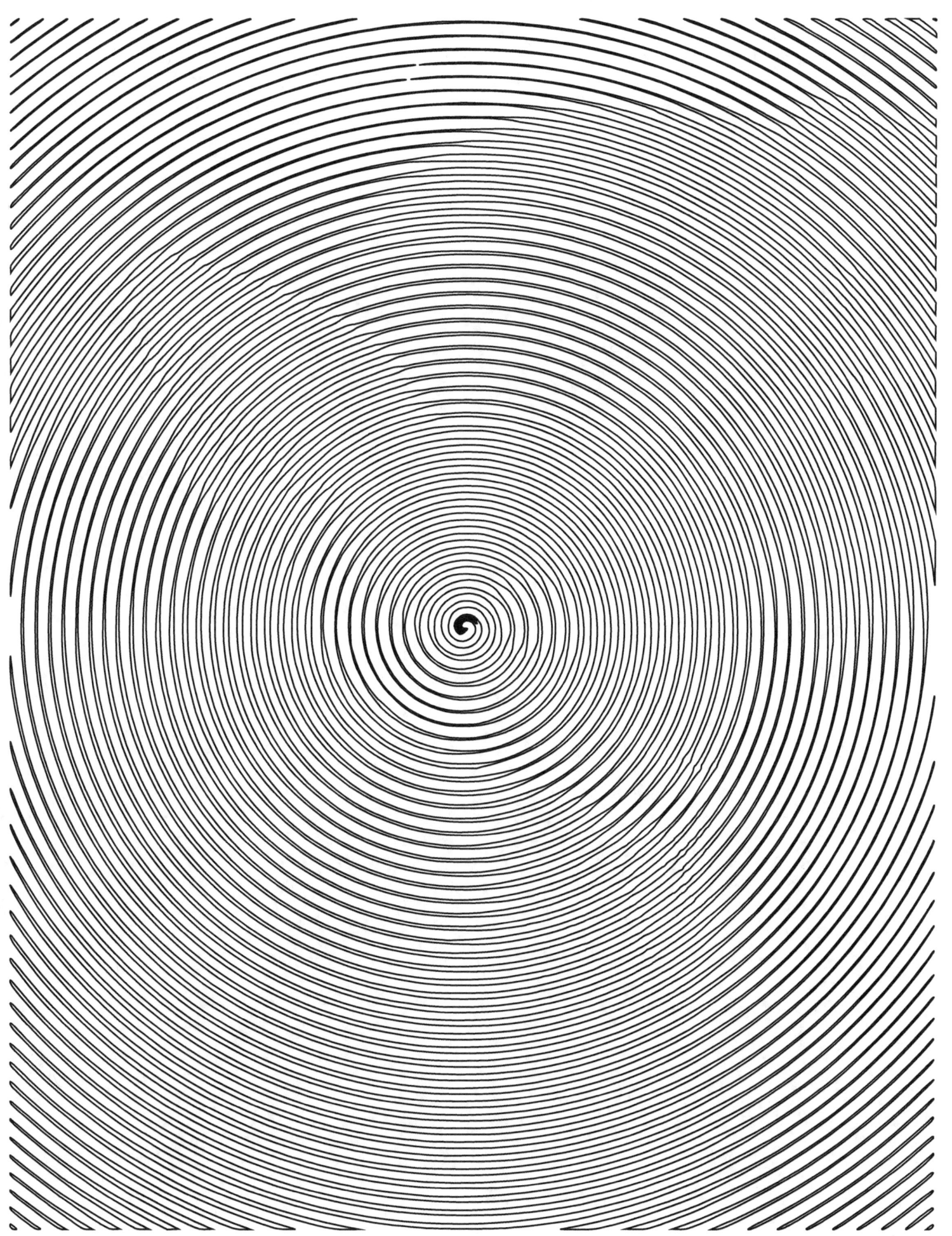

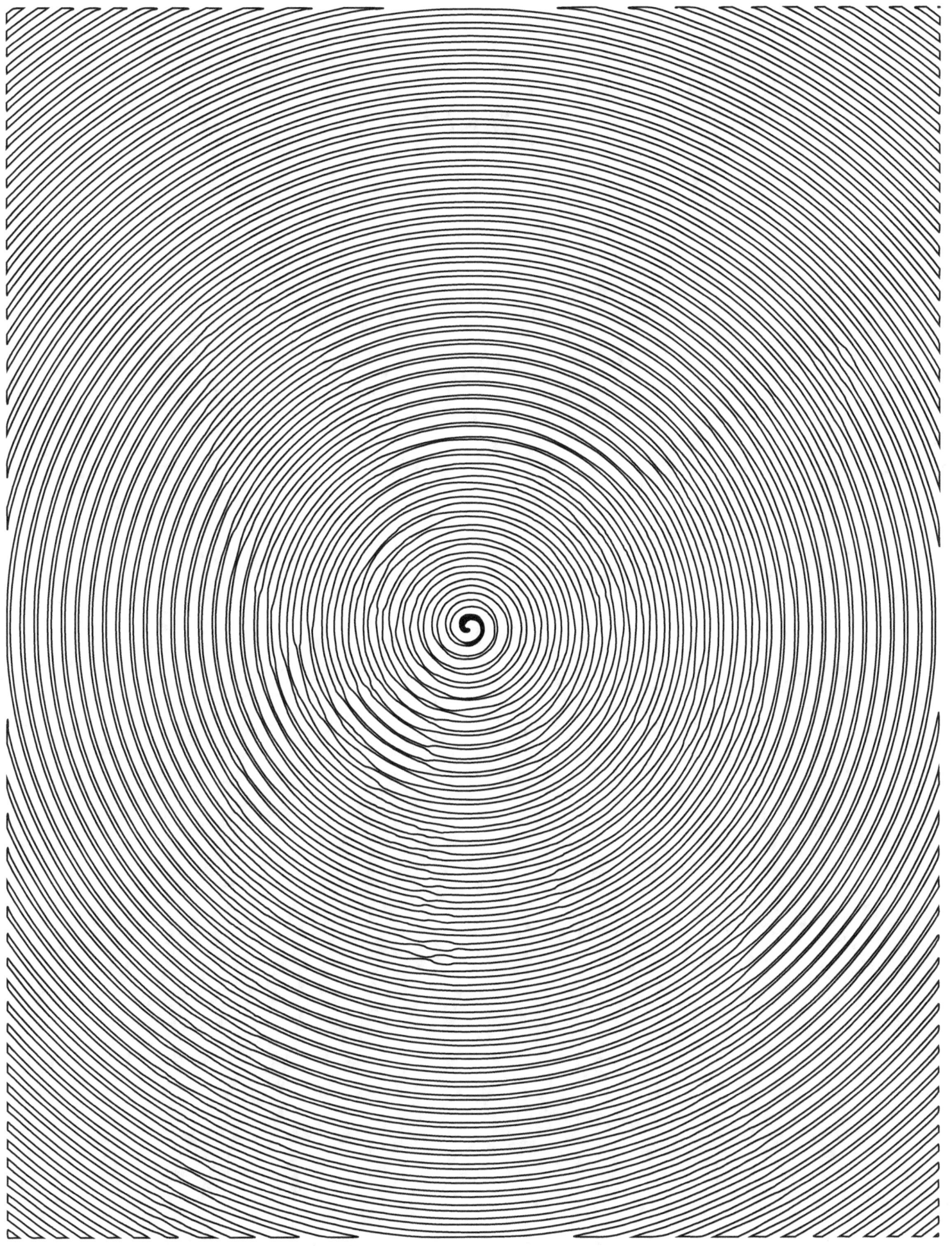

- HINTS -

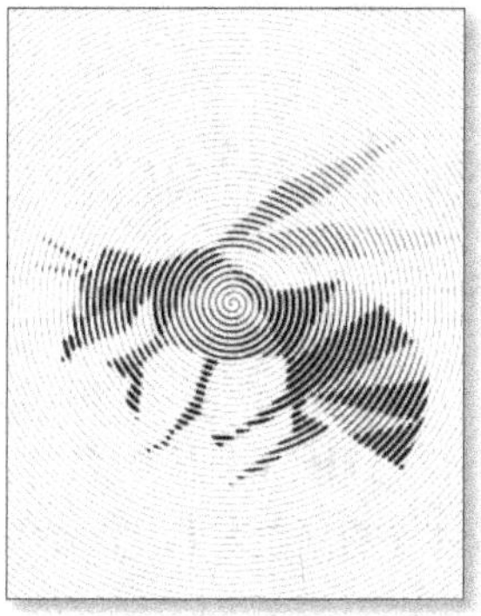

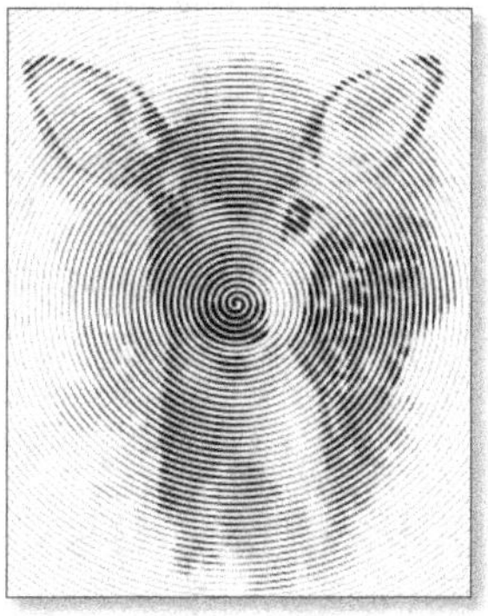

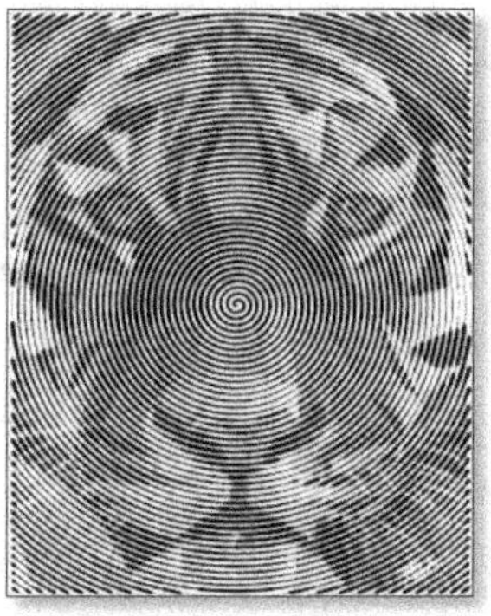

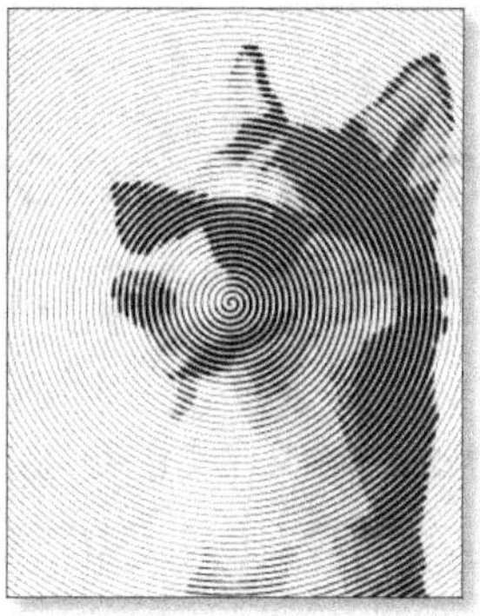

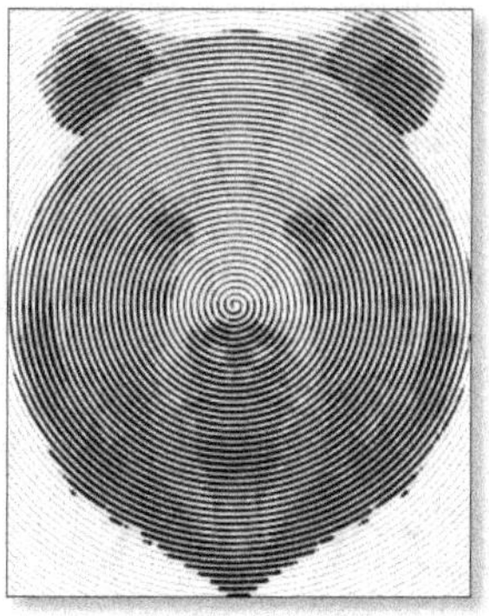

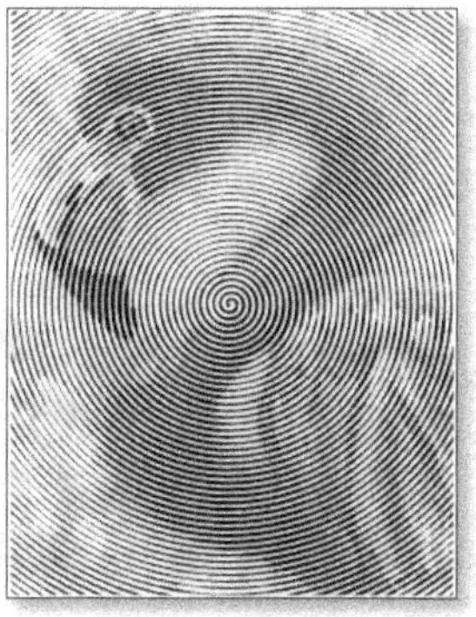

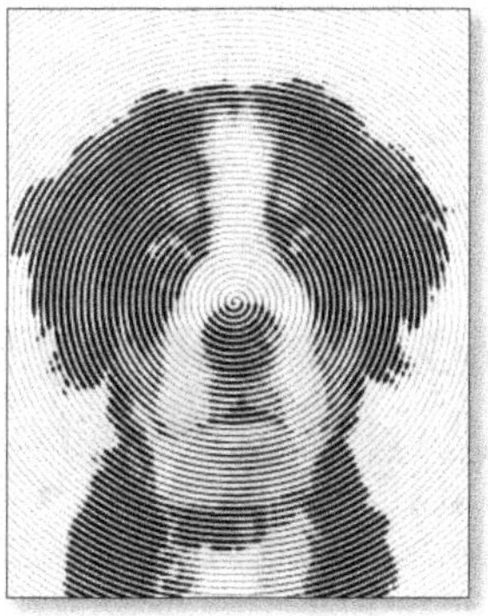

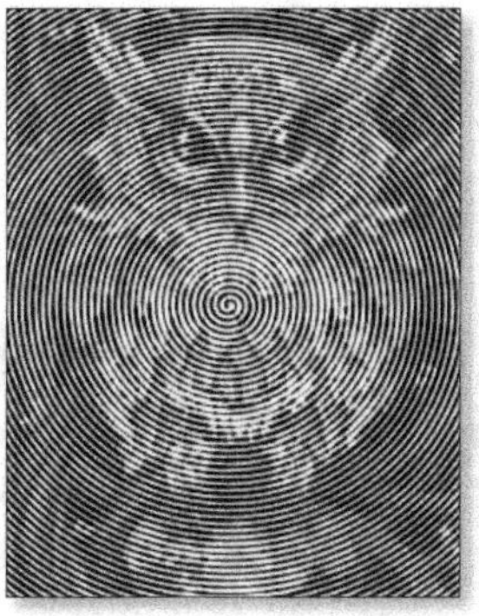

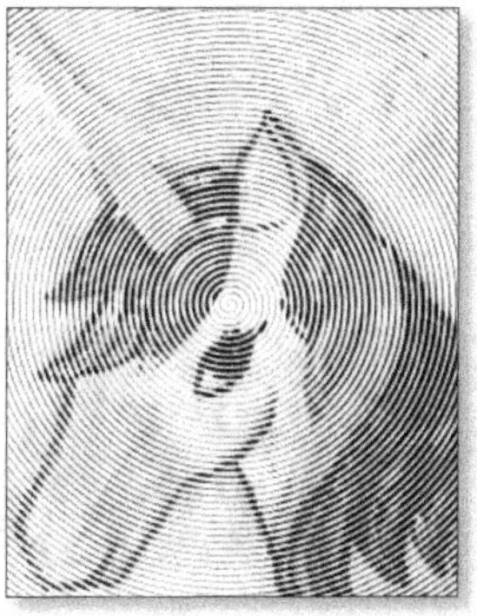

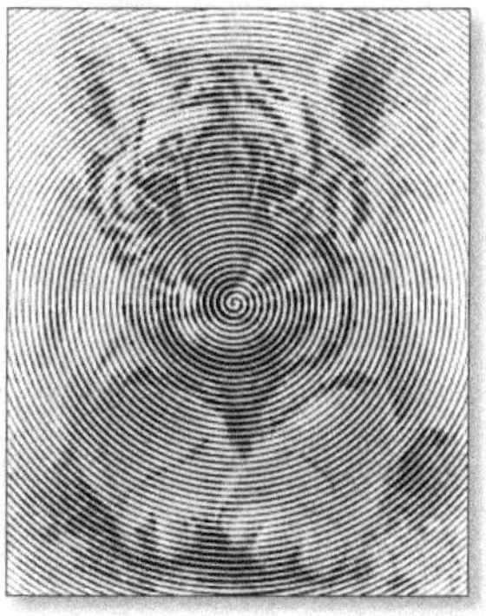

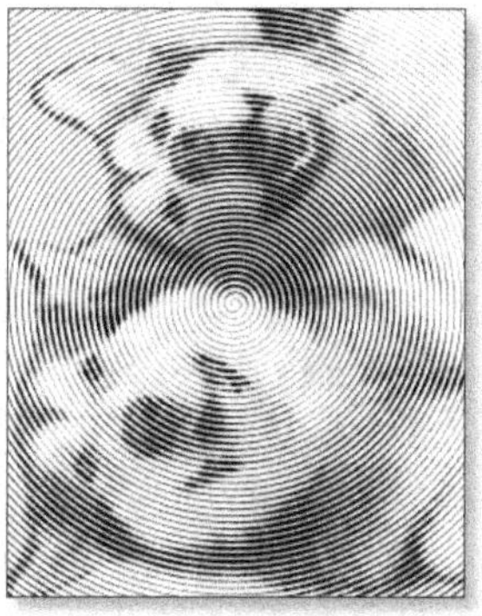

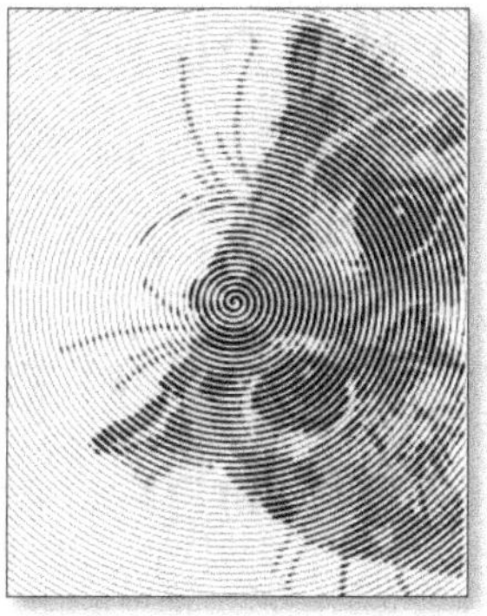

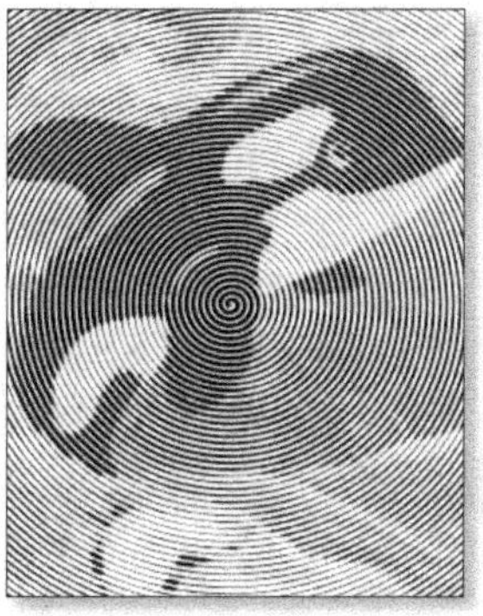

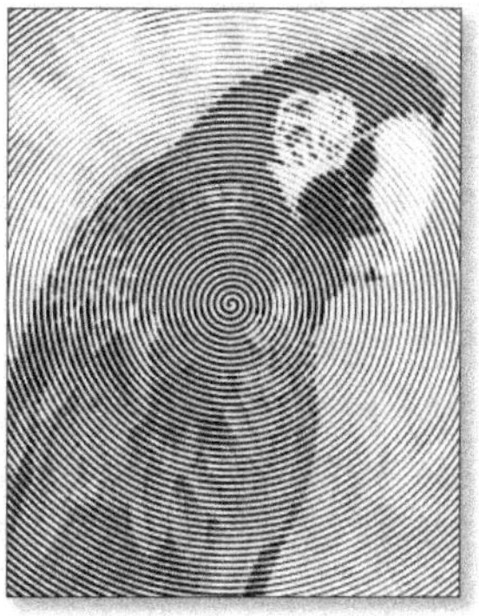

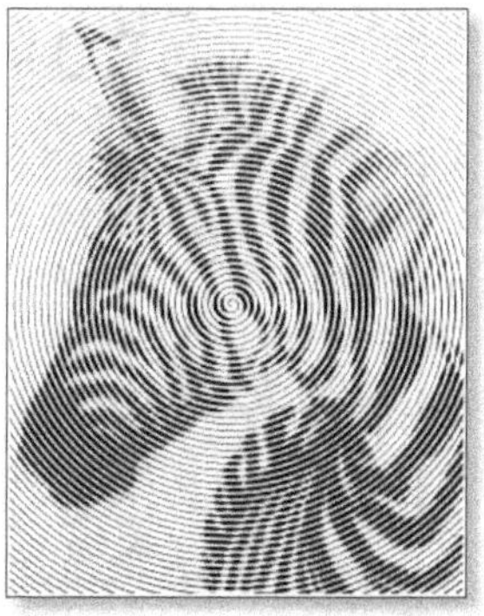

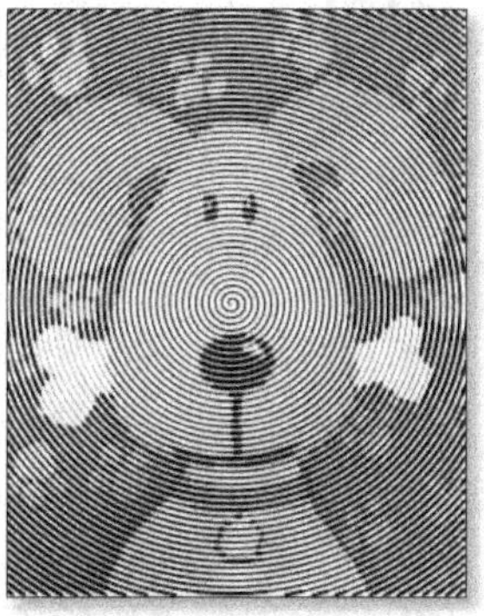

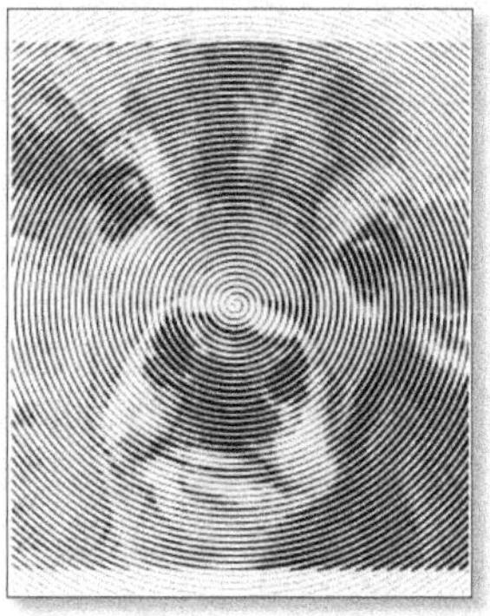

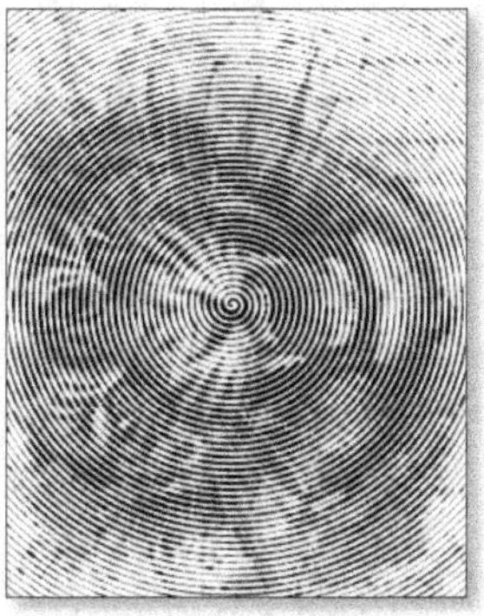

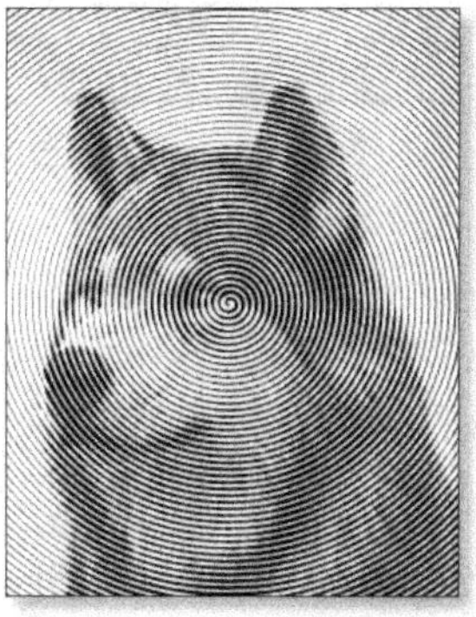

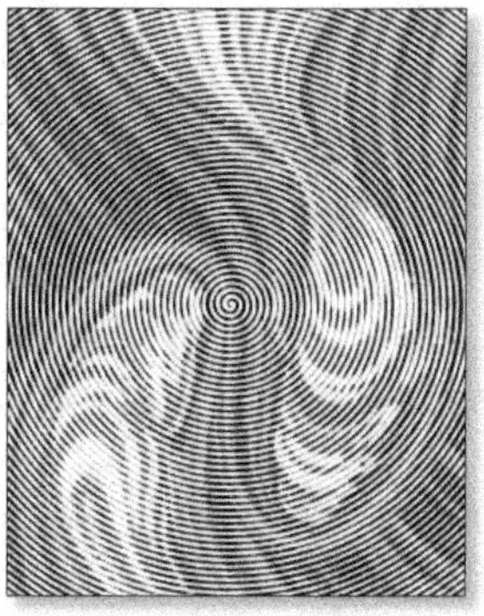

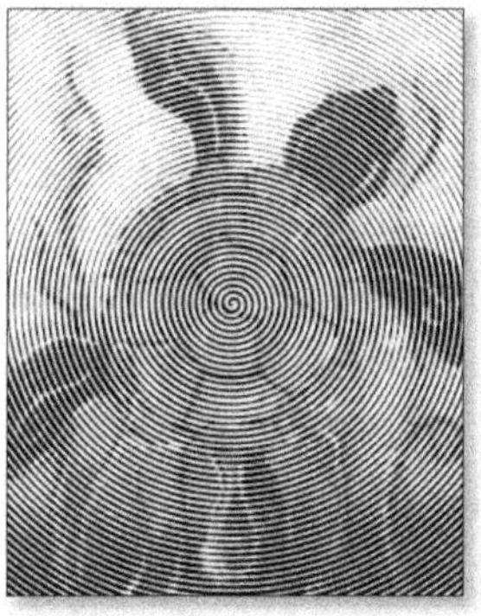

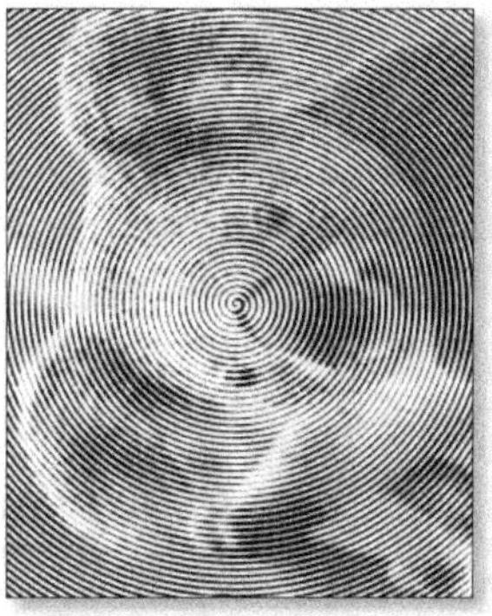

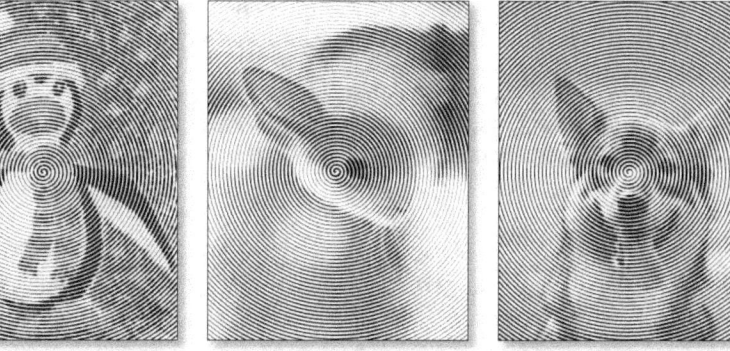

Thank you for choosing Bright-Ideas Paper Publishing.
We hope you enjoy coloring your pages.

Feel free to share your colored pages with friends, family, and within the coloring community. Copying or otherwise reproducing uncolored pages is strictly forbidden.

A Special Request
LEAVE YOUR AMAZON REVIEWS

Show your support for us and help other colorists discover our artwork.

Simply find this book on Amazon, scroll to the reviews section, and click "Write a customer review"

Thank you for your purchases and reviews!

Copyright © 2020 Bright-Ideas Paper Publishing.
All Rights Reserved.

No part of this book may be reproduced or transmitted in any form or by any means, electronic or mechanical, including photocopying, recording or by any information storage and retrieval system, without written permission from the publisher.

The information provided within this book is for general informational purposes only. While we try to keep the information up-to-date and correct, there are no representations or warranties, express or implied, about the completeness, accuracy, reliability, suitability or availability with respect to the information, products, services, or related graphics contained in this book for any purpose.

Have a question or concern? Let us know
Bright-Ideas Paper Publishing | Bright.IdeasPaperPublishing@gmail.com